LADY NO

ALSO BY KIM HYESOON

Phantom Pain Wings

A Drink of Red Mirror

Autobiography of Death

Poor Love Machine

I'm OK, I'm Pig!

Sorrowtoothpaste Mirrorcream

All the Garbage of the World, Unite!

Mommy Must be a Fountain of Feathers

When the Plug Gets Unplugged

Anxiety of Words

LADY NO

TRANSLATED FROM THE KOREAN BY JACK SAEBYOK JUNG

DRAWINGS BY FI JAE LEE

KIM HYESOON

ecco
An Imprint of HarperCollins*Publishers*

Without limiting the exclusive rights of any author, contributor or the publisher of this publication, any unauthorized use of this publication to train generative artificial intelligence (AI) technologies is expressly prohibited. HarperCollins also exercise their rights under Article 4(3) of the Digital Single Market Directive 2019/790 and expressly reserve this publication from the text and data mining exception.

LADY NO. Copyright © 2026 by Kim Hyesoon. English translation copyright © 2026 by Jack Saebyok Jung. All rights reserved. No part of this book may be used or reproduced in any manner whatsoever without written permission except in the case of brief quotations embodied in critical articles and reviews. For information, address HarperCollins Publishers, 195 Broadway, New York, NY 10007. In Europe, HarperCollins Publishers, Macken House, 39/40 Mayor Street Upper, Dublin 1, D01 C9W8, Ireland.

HarperCollins books may be purchased for educational, business, or sales promotional use. For information, please email the Special Markets Department at SPsales@harpercollins.com.

harpercollins.com

Ecco® and HarperCollins® are trademarks of HarperCollins Publishers.

Originally published as 않아는 이렇게 말했다 in Korea in 2022 by Munhakdongne Publishing Group.

This book is published with the support of the Literature Translation Institute of Korea (LTI Korea).

This book is supported in part by an award from the National Endowment for the Arts.

FIRST US EDITION

Designed by Alison Bloomer
Art by Fi Jae Lee

Library of Congress Cataloging-in-Publication Data has been applied for.

ISBN 978-0-06-344668-7

Printed in the United States of America

26 27 28 29 30 LBC 5 4 3 2 1

FOR THE CHILDREN OF AEROK

CONTENTS

Translator's Introduction   *xiii*

MARCH

From Aerok   2
The Body of a Woman   3
Life Experts   4
Proverb Teachers   6
Ear Patients   8
Companion Trunk   11
Chili Con Carne   13
The Past Not Yet Here   15
Life of a Stage Director   16
Escaping   17
René Magritte and the Charles Bonnet Syndrome   18
To Not Rot After Death   20
Aerok Fiction Factory   21
The Name of Poetry   24
Inside of Winning   25
Cute Grandpa   26
The Lips of the Songs   27
Fiction and Poetry   29
Out-of-Date Genres   31
The Privilege of Bleeding   34
Seeing the Multi-Genre Audience   35
Paying Respect to the Food   36
Last Ounce of Strength   38

APRIL

Arctic   42
Lady No's France   43
A Writing Script Only Women Use   45
The Worst Shame in Life   46
Thus Spoke Lady No   48
No Words to Express the Body   49
Roger Corman   51
Barely Light Barely White Barely Right   52
Emergency Room   54
Avant-Garde Poet   56
Poop   58
Sentence Endings for Fathers and Men   60
Document Human   61
Mozart   63
Living Fiction   65
The Desk Clock in the Main Buddha Hall   67
A Dialogue from Apichatpong Weerasethakul's
Syndromes and a Century   68
A Message from Lady No   70

MAY

Drizzling April   72
Metaphor Ban   73
Easter   74
Vacation   76
Once It Becomes Words, It Disappears   78
I Live in Aerok   80

JUNE

Tears of Everest   82
Time Eraser   83
Exhibitions of a Female Artist and a Male Artist   84
The Soul of an Object   88
Devotion Index   89

Time Returns as an Itch 91
By the River Ouse 94
Thin Country 96
Far Beyond 98
Mammal 100
Imported Alibi 102
The Sun King's Chairs 105
Circle 106
Yet Unborn 108
The Voice of a Wart 110
Living in Leaving 113
Questions 115
The Host of Death 117
Mothers 119
Witch-Type Poet 120
Asymptotic Curve 124
Lecture and Protest 126

JULY

Vowels 128
That Woman's Kitchen 131
Even In Front of Would-Be Writers 133
When Will We Finish This Practice? 135
On a Razzle-Dazzle Makeshift Stage 138
The Face of a Quilt 140
Mothers Despise Doing It Too 142
Tearstain Growth Rings 143
Oh, Honest Poem! 145
Rational Number's Infinity 147
Flowers of the World 149
The Song of an Empty Room 151
Rain of Poems 153
Like Two Planets in Love 154
Poetry Workshop 156
Cooking Verb 158

The Infinite Accelerator of Anxious Universe   159
A Poem Is a Tree   162
Underground Loneliness   164
Manhole Humanity   167
Empty Frame   169
Arriving at a Form   171
Pontius Pilate Governors   174
Nightmare Soup   177
Sylvia and Mrs. Brown's Bread   178
An Aspiring Fiction Writer   181
The Names of Sardines and Mallards   183
To My Mind   186

AUGUST

Piano and Camel   188
Revolutionary's New Job   189
Self-Appointed Measurement Standard of All Creation   191
Waiting for My Very Own Giraffe   195
A Song That Came and Went as a Hum   197
The 'once~' Side of the World   199
Words of an Object   201
Disappearing Genre   203
Cowardly Old Woman   205
Fish with Shaven Heads   207
We Had Already Used Her Up   209
What Do I Do When I Can't Forget   211
Father Is Growing   213
Star Giver and Star Receiver   214
Bean Dishes of Many Countries   215
One Day I Will Cast Away Personification   217
Choice   219
Phone Call   225
Princesses in Formaldehyde   226
Are You a Member?   228
Audacious Resolve   229

SEPTEMBER

DMZ Green   232
Is Reunification Possible Without War?   234
Recipes During Bombardment   236
Entrance Exam   237
Teacher Buys Me a Meal   239
Virginhood and Motherhood   241
North Mountain   243
Rodriguez and Rodriguez   245
Like Fresh Food   248
Silence Producing Machines   249
Laudation   251
We Need Martyrdom in Modern Too   252
We Protect Strangers' Sleep   254
I I I I   256
Bookstore of My Maternal Grandfather   258
Walking in New York   261
Yeti   262
To Feed and Keep Alive the Rhythm   263
Holidays   265
Let Me Heal You   266
Scary Community   268
Rattle   270
Migraine   273
Humiliation   275
The Role Assigned to Lady No in This World   277
Conductor of Fate   278
Shaking Minari   279
Teacher and Student   280
KAL   281

OCTOBER

Idolatry Bibimbap   286
Fishes and Stories About Families   288
Three Women   289

Daeheung Temple 290
My Name and Your Names 292
Wedding March 294
Poet's Name 296
Lady No's Wife 298
Death Metal and an Orphan Girl 299
A Spine Called Solitude 300
Why Do Old People Become Children? 301
What Is Inspiration 303
If Only I Had a Console, Too 305
What Is My Body Made Out Of 306
Leviathan of Lady No 307
Arrogant Lord English 308
Old Daughters 310
The Peaceful Reign of King Sentimental the Great 311
Infected with Future 314
February Zombie 316
Genre of Servility 318
Lady No Does Not Want to Be Marked 320
Hospital Ward 322
If There Are Realms for Each Part of Speech 323
The Place Now 325
Mom's Knitting 328

EPILOGUE

Ennui 332
Music's Existence 334
Earth-Smelling Keystrokes 336
The Roommate of Lady No 338
The Shoes You Wear When You Enter Your Dreams 340
Fasting 341

Poet's Afterword 343
Artist's Afterword 345

TRANSLATOR'S INTRODUCTION

Under a regime whose violent whims could ruin lives in a matter of hours—where secret-police-in-all-but-name arrested anyone deemed ideologically threatening—Kim Hyesoon began her literary career in the late 1970s, as an editor at a South Korean publishing house. This was a period of South Korea's history ruled by military dictatorships, propped up by Cold War alignments and fervent anticommunism, with escalating tensions over free speech and the suppression of dissent by those in power. And to live and write under that regime was to hear again and again the word "No." As in: "No, you cannot write this. No, you cannot discuss this. No, you cannot even think this."

Day after day, Kim painstakingly polished manuscripts, only to have entire passages vanish under the government censors' thick markers, reduced to ominous blocks of black ink. At one point, after helping to edit and publish the Korean translation of a biography of American labor organizer Mary G. Harris Jones—better known as Mother Jones—Kim was summoned to a police station. There, the interrogators demanded the home address and phone number of the book's translator; when Kim refused to cooperate, they slapped her across the face repeatedly, a total of seven times. Unwilling to be silenced by the brutality, Kim herself began writing at the close of the 1970s. And indeed she would go on to write seven poems about the incident, one for each blow.[*]

Early on as a poet, Kim honed a haunting, elliptical style charged with rhythmic, tightly woven lines. One might imagine her work as a

---

[*] Kim Hyesoon (김혜순), "Siin sŏjŏng" (시인 서정) [Poet's Introduction], in *Ŏnŭ pyŏl ŭi chiok* (어느 별의 지옥) [The Hell of That Star], *Munhakgwa Jiseongsa Siin-sŏn* R12 (Seoul: Munhakgwa Jiseongsa, 2017). Originally published 1988 by Cheongha.

kind of witch's brew, infused with dark spells, grotesque tenderness, and occluded truths. Kim once called herself a "witch," for the way her poetry's eerie aura straddles the boundary between everyday reality and an occult disturbance, asserting a defiantly feminist stance. In those first works, she wrote of death not as a moment of final closure but as a continuous dissolution of life—an edge where bodies collapse, energies scatter, and the line between life and afterlife recedes. In this poet's liminality of being and nothingness, we find mother and daughter, father and state, living and dead, normalcy and nightmare, each pair reflected again and again. Literary critic Hwang Hyeon-san* described Kim's poetry as a series of mirrors facing each other, creating abyssal holes on each other's surfaces through infinite reflections of "twoness" that reveal both the poet and the world.

When the mid-1980s arrived, South Koreans rose against unjust power and secured democracy through protests and sacrifices that transformed the political landscape. An economic "miracle" followed—then collapse, then recovery, and so on. Along the way, a new kind of "No" took hold across the land: there was no time to slow down in a nation driven by breakneck market expansion. Everyone had to hustle. Everyone had to conform. Kim Hyesoon, nevertheless, kept writing. She turned her gaze outward to the city of Seoul and its expanding labyrinth, a half-manmade, half-natural desert, every bit as brutal as the old regime but far more relentless in its demands for endless productivity.

The death Kim wrote about in her earliest works is still the same death that saturates this new cityscape: an ongoing performance of unraveling, a continuum where life's boundaries are unstable. It is a dance that no longer needs to tiptoe around censors but must now dodge the crushing weight of a globalized market and its demands for speed and productivity. Her lines, filled with chanting cadences, sometimes evoke

---

* Hwang Hyeon-san (황현산), "Ttal ŭi samak kwa ŏmŏni ŭi Sŏul – Na ŭi Upanishad, Sŏul kkaji ŭi Kim Hyesoon" [The Daughter's Desert and the Mother's Seoul: My Upanishad, Kim Hyesoon to Seoul], in *Mal gwa sigan ŭi kip'i* (말과 시간의 깊이) [The Depth of Words and Time] (Seoul: Munhakgwa Jiseongsa, 2002), 277–311.

gruesome images, yet they just as often suggest a fierce resilience, pointing to a future form of life that remains nameless but undeniably present beneath the surface.* In so doing, her poems partake of a shamanic resonance: the voice of a mudang, a Korean shaman, calling up ancestors, gods, and the lost in a rite that merges private trauma with larger societal cataclysms.

Kim's poetry remains a testament to what language can do in a world designed to say "No" at every turn. Starting from the dictatorship of the 1970s, she conjured elliptical movements in her verses that outmaneuvered censors. Today, in the restrictive grind of modern society, she writes and rewrites the boundaries of poetry, creating an emotional vocabulary for seeing and naming the precariousness beneath the gleaming surfaces. Readers join her in that corridor of infinite mirrors, where censored lines might find a second life in translation and no amount of capitalist frenzy can finally white out the shadows that Kim's poetry uncovers.

INTRODUCING LADY NO

Out of this decades-long engagement with censorship, transformation, and creative resistance comes *Lady No*, a volume that stands apart as perhaps Kim Hyesoon's most openly hybrid work and a documentation of her first and only work of digital performance art. In 2014, after Kim's stature as a major force in contemporary Korean poetry was well established, she posted anonymously for eight months on the blog of Munhakdongne, a major South Korean publisher, using the persona 않아 (pronounced *ahn-ah*). This pseudonym, itself a form of negation in Korean, already signals Kim's playful yet defiant stance toward conventions—linguistic, literary,

---

* Parts of this reading are from an earlier lecture I've given: Kim Hyesoon and Don Mee Choi, *T. S. Eliot Memorial Reading*, lecture at Houghton Library, Harvard University, October 2, 2023. Introductory remarks by Jack Jung. The text of this lecture is available online: Jack Jung, "Visiting Poets: Jack Jung on Kim Hyesoon," *Poetry Society of America*.

and social. Alongside Kim's texts, her daughter, the award-winning artist Fi Jae Lee, featured a selection of her extant drawings, visually mirroring the eerie power of Kim's words.

During this eight-month period, the Sewol ferry disaster struck, claiming the lives of 304 souls—the majority of them high school students. The country reeled in grief, and Kim's postings halted for forty-nine days as mourning laid bare systemic failures in South Korean society. Eventually, the posts resumed and in 2016 these 179 writings—poems, prose poems, opinion columns, travelogues, and more—were gathered into a single volume under the original Korean title 않아는 이렇게 말했다 (*ahn-ahneun yirutke malhatda*), or "Thus Spoke *Ahn-ah*." It alludes parodically to Nietzsche's *Thus Spoke Zarathustra*, suggesting that like Zarathustra, Kim's speaker—or "Lady No," as she is now known in English—has come to proclaim a truthsaying that both defies and reinvents the world.

As in much of Kim's oeuvre, the speaker here straddles a space between body and spirit, calling into question "normal" definitions of poetry and prose. Indeed, Kim labels the text *shisanmun*—poetry-prose, or po-prose, "minus poetry, minus prose." She insists that it cannot be neatly filed under any one genre. In *Lady No*, the oracular, bodily, and political all intertwine with the mundane details of life in Seoul and the fictional land of "Aerok," a mirror-version of Korea where the country's anxieties, gender politics, and media obsessions are magnified.

Initially considered for English publication as *Thus Spoke n't*, then *Thus Spoke No*, and at one point known as *Thus Spoke Lady No*, the book now simply appears as *Lady No*. This shifting title, much like the pseudonym ahn-ah, evokes the idea of negation—of refusing established categories, refusing compliance, and, in the final iteration, personifying resistance as a figure of feminist critique. The choice of *Lady No* also pays homage to Don Mee Choi's translation of Kim Hyesoon's *Autobiography of Death* (New Directions 2018), in which a poem titled "Lord No" (translating 아님) portrays a patriarchal, almost god-like persona in a shamanic incantatory chant that could either be for or against this figure. By inverting "Lord No" into "Lady No," this English title claims its own radical feminine power, foregrounding a direct challenge to the very structures of authority embedded in the original poem.

Far more colloquial, even slangy, than much of her previous writing, *Lady No* thus exposes a directness in Kim's voice that Anglophone readers may not have seen before. She writes about popular television, the aspirations and disappointments of a creative writing professor, glimpses of ongoing social injustices—and she does so with the same vital sense of imagination that characterizes her more iconically surreal poems. Yet in these pages, the poet also hints at the "source code" behind her worldview, showing how everyday experience and sociopolitical trauma fuel her explorations of the body, desire, violence, art, and the strange boundaries between them.

One key editorial choice in this English translation has been to restore the sequence of the original blog posts, rather than follow the rearranged sequence as appears in the original Korean edition. This decision allows readers to experience in "real time" how the Sewol ferry disaster tragically interrupted the serialization; in the days after the accident, the blog featured a message from Lady No that expressed the unutterable shock of the national tragedy.

Kim Hyesoon's work began to be introduced in English around 2012. Since then, her works have been honored with multiple awards in North America, including the Griffin Poetry Prize and National Book Critics Circle Award. Kim Hyesoon's broader global recognition is intertwined with the work of Don Mee Choi, her longtime translator into English. In her translations, Don Mee Choi refuses to "smooth out" Kim's dissonances, favoring instead a translation mode that peels away colonial overtones and refuses to domesticate the poems. In this sense, translation itself becomes political. By bringing Kim's language into English on Korean terms—retaining its uncanny leaps, refusing to flatten its strangeness—Don Mee Choi shows that translation can be an anti-colonial practice.*

Through this synergy, Kim Hyesoon's longtime refusal of censorship and Don Mee Choi's refusal of imperial linguistic frames form a deeper reflection of twoness, an endless corridor of mirrors in which the poet and translator, Korean and English, body and ruin, mother and father appear. Honoring the fruitful collaboration between Kim Hyesoon and Don Mee Choi that has so deeply shaped Anglophone perceptions of Kim's poetry, my own approach to translating *Lady No* is similar, but diverges at certain stylistic junctures. Where Don Mee Choi emphasizes a radical, idiosyncratic syntax that foregrounds rupture, I sometimes focus on a direct, immediate resonance in English—leaning into colloquial or comedic textures that match the text's diary-like flow. If Don Mee's approach was pure poetry, in mine I've let trappings of English prose creep its way into that poetry. I believe that both methods share the same ultimate goal of preserving Kim's fierce strangeness, yet each indicates a distinct interpretive path, revealing just how multifaceted Kim Hyesoon's writing truly is.

American readers immersed in ongoing debates about what constitutes poetry, or how the lyric essay intersects with fiction, will find *Lady No* a fascinating case. Many pieces here might be called lyric essays in an American context, or perhaps creative nonfiction, yet Kim Hyesoon doesn't regard them as poems either. Instead, as mentioned before, she conceives a fresh category—a "not-poetry and not-prose" that reassembles both forms into something new. By calling it poetry-prose (*shisanmun*), she acknowledges an impulse to break with old structures while still paying homage to the elasticity of Korean literary tradition.

Lady No is, ultimately, Kim Hyesoon's clarion call on the page: an insistence on negation as creative method, a declaration of resistance to

---

* Don Mee Choi, *Translation Is a Mode = Translation Is an Anti-neocolonial Mode* (Brooklyn, NY: Ugly Duckling Presse, 2020).

the illusions of progress and prosperity that overshadow real lives, and a deeply personal mourning for those who suffer in such illusions' wake. Its final English title conveys an unmistakable refusal—an unwavering, embodied "No" that resonates with Kim's longstanding critique of patriarchal and political oppression, the same refusal she maintained under dictatorship, the same she carried into the global hypercapitalism of the present. Just as "Aerok" functions as a twisted palindrome of Korea—a land at once different and strangely the same—so too might we conceive of Aerok as a mirror for American life, reflecting back our own intensifying injustices and psychic fissures. In a world increasingly riddled with obstacles to free thought and genuine empathy, *Lady No* stands as a testament that no single state, no single genre, and no single vantage can contain Kim Hyesoon's visionary reach. Indeed, she summons us into that corridor of mirrors facing mirrors, where each reflection discloses another uncharted dimension of ourselves and our societies.

APRIL 2026
Jack Saebyok Jung

MARCH

FROM AEROK

From Aerok, I write.

Barely, here I write.

Here I will live, and here I will die.

Barely, I will stay until the time comes to move on.

Along streets lined with beauty parlors, boarding houses, hospitals, banks, restaurants, cell phone shops, and fruit stalls, I stay awhile and return to write once more.

How many number of bus rides, and how many number of books, and how many number of films, and how many number of drinks, and how many number of visits to my mother, and how many number of tears . . . await.

Here, in Aerok. Beyond 'Nothing more to desire.' Beyond 'Can no longer live.'

In this makeshift stage of a city, a razzle-dazzle of hollow shells.

In this makeshift stage of a country.

Straightening the hair of my sweater where pink fuzz rises.

The loneliness of a star called Earth floating in the cosmos.

Clinging to a corner of this lonely star, the country of Aerok cradles her tiny skeletal mountains. They are like so many insects banished from outer space.

Like the intoxication with echoes from a well with no water, this writing, is it to be drunk with loneliness?

Here

to live.

To love.

THE BODY OF A WOMAN

While flipping through the Bible, fooling around, I found a verse: ". . . is there any taste in the white of an egg?" (Job 6:6).

Reminiscent of the white of an egg.

Finely minced seaweed.

Minced famine crop, like chamma.

Minced onion, garlic, and cabbage.

Like the cartilage in a knee joint.

Like my cerebellum and cerebrum.

Sticky and fishy.

A substance that women frequently secrete.

Pink.

"Can that which is unsavory be eaten?"

Inside a brain that is like whipped egg white, I am piling up memories that no one craves.

What can Lady No do to turn herself into a delicacy anyone would want to eat? Will meditation work? She thinks about it.

LIFE EXPERTS

Memorized every subway station in order.
Knows the names of every Aerok mountain peak.
Swiftly organizes a box of toothpicks
(can even pick up a thousand acupuncture needles all at once).
Efficiently buses numerous trays.
Carries countless steins.
Excels at peeling chestnuts quickly.
Arranges lunchboxes with speed.
Transplants hair follicles.
Crafts pretty dumplings.
Knits fast.

Presenting the number one experts of their respective fields, this television program seems to be persuading us that these life experts are truly fulfilled, that they are exemplary models for our lives, that they know happiness, that they have grasped eternal unchanging values, that they are untouched by melancholy, that their souls have become one with their labor work. When she watches this show, Lady No also yearns to quickly become an expert in something. Even something like spitting farther than anyone else or being the best organizer of desks. Beside each expert sits a radio, chattering incessantly, silent only in sleep. This radio bends time into a loop, making it impossible to get outside of time. So Lady No ponders this. She delves into her thoughts, even though thinking is the gateway to her anxiety. These experts, who became what they are after exhausting their bodies every day. Who must grab one hundred toothpicks with one hand just to continue existing in this world. Their souls have become one with their radios. They heed the radio's voice, the DJ who incessantly preaches hope, and they nod at his words. Does harboring hope propel us to grasp a hundred chopsticks over a hundred toothpicks? First, let's listen to the radio. And endure the DJ's awkward prattle, the radio host's jokes. For now.

PROVERB TEACHERS

Proverb teacher 1 stepped forward, and everyone went wild.
Proverb teacher 2 stepped forward, and everyone went wild.
Proverb teacher 3 stepped forward, and everyone went wild.

The proverb teachers ascended the podium and proverbed proverbs.
They proverbed these proverbs, campaigning for election or not.
Busy as they are crafting these proverbs, when do the proverb teachers work?
Comedians, too, proverbed proverbs in their proverbial jokes.
Singers proverbed their proverbial songs with proverbs.

This is how you eat
This is how you sleep
This is how you love
This is how you think

This is what to do when you're jobless
This is what to do when you're penniless

Lady No finds the endless proverbs from these teachers intolerable.
She is fed up with their cold illuminations, like neon lights that can't burn.

Consider one proverb teacher who addressed a person in deep agony:
"You grow as much as you are in pain," (you die if you are in pain).
"Pain defines you," (you die if you endure pain).
"Embrace all pain," (you die eventually).

Those who don't recite proverbs have become rarities.
Many have set aside work to devote themselves to proverbs.
Dressed for their jobs, they set out to proverb.
Terrifying people like proverbs.

In a neighboring country, there lived a man.
He spread so much laughter on a comedy show.
He was full of passion on TV, as if he were willing to die for triviality.
He became an actor-director and sprayed bullets in his films.
Sparing neither the innocent nor the righteous.
His room flickered brightly with the sounds and flames of killing.
Perhaps he couldn't bear proverbs any longer.

See how, standing around a deathbed,
They proverb their proverbs in proverbs
To the one who is dying.
"Journey to the light! Stay the course! Don't return!"

EAR PATIENTS

Ear patients lie on canopy beds veiled with drapes.
It is just after lunchtime.
(During brief breaks from work, they come here to be ear patients for a few dozen minutes.)
A doctor of traditional medicine moves around behind the drapes,
placing acupuncture needles into the patients' ears while engaging in small talk.

"I hear crickets."
"I hear the scratch of a chair on the floor."
"I hear the pressing of keypads."
"A bug is crying out."
"I want to identify that bird, I really want to."
"I hear the croaking of toads."
"A train is passing by."
Lady No answers that she hears a passcode being pressed somewhere as a door is unlocked, and that she writes out its melody in her head.
(How many levels am I hearing the elevator ascend in an hour? My count goes: 1st floor, 2nd floor, 3rd floor . . . 595th floor, 9,592nd floor . . . charging beyond the galaxy.)
From an adjacent bed, a voice remarks that the music they hear during the day lingers until sleep takes them.
At Bright Sounds Traditional Medicine Center, people are resting behind their drapes, acupuncture needles protruding from their ears, each hearing different sounds.

"In a few days, I'll present a draft proposal."
"I've been under review for several days now."
"I have no idea why this is happening," Lady No lies.

Behind drapes are people with tasks due in a few days.
Lying there, they resemble pink fetuses, brimming with sounds.
They are attuned to what their ears are saying.

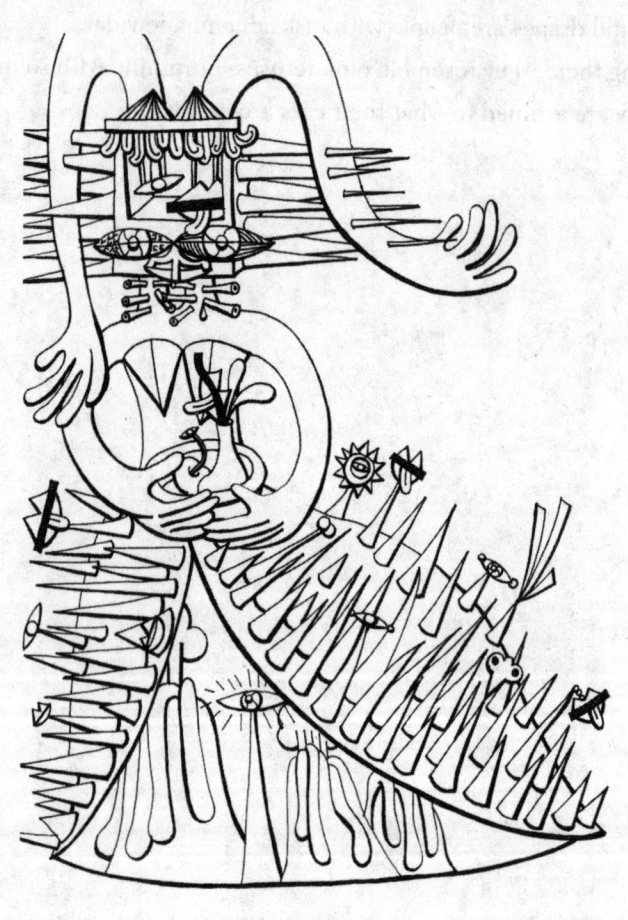

COMPANION TRUNK

Among the poets invited to a poetry festival, there was a woman poet from Eritrea. Eritrea became an independent country in 1993.
    The Eritrean flag bears the colors green, red, and blue.

Green for agriculture and forests,
Red for the blood shed for independence,
Blue for the Red Sea,
And the emblem of the olive branch for hope—

This is what I was told each color represents.
    This poet had endured torture and abuse in Eritrean prisons. Subsequently, she lived as an undocumented immigrant in various European nations until Italy recently granted her asylum. Everywhere she went, this woman poet took her trunk with her. Even when she was told to leave it in her room, she clung to it. She even carried it onstage as she recited her poems, like a child contestant in a singing competition. She refused to be separated from her trunk. The trunk was tethered to her as though it were a beloved, obese pup. She lugged it and dragged it to tea shops and evening dance excursions with fellow poets. On one occasion, she retrieved five small stones from her trunk. She showed us a game of jackstones and invited anyone familiar with it to join her. Surprisingly, everyone there was acquainted with the game. The only difference between us was a unique flourish, a respective twist of the wrist marking each of our final moves. Poets from Afghanistan, India, and South Aerok emerged as the highest scorers in this tournament of jackstones.

When the woman poet from Eritrea ascended the stage with her trunk and began her recital, she read her poetry. No, she howled:

rorororororororororororo rorororororororo

The sound resembled a bird trilling in Eritrea's forests vibrating from a tongue like a pink petal. No translation was necessary, no English subtitles required. It was the lament of a bird crying from beyond the system we call literature.

CHILI CON CARNE

I will tell you how to make chili con carne.

First, you add garlic and Worcestershire sauce to finely minced beef, then you stir-fry it in butter.

Then, add diced jalapenos, diced bell peppers, and diced onions, and keep stir-frying.

Next, add diced tomatoes and continue stir-frying.

Then, incorporate boiled kidney beans and keep stir-frying.

Stir-fry.
Stir-fry.
Stir-fry.

Finally, add chili powder (with cumin) and boil it.

Boil.
Boil.
Boil.

Cook until the dish resembles someone's insides. A pink broth will emerge.

Beans will morph into beef, and beef into beans. Onions will release their juices until they vanish. Continue stir-frying until all this occurs.

This is the dish that Zorg prepares with a nickel-silver pot in the opening scene of Djian's film, 37°2 *le matin*.

Chili con carne is now ready to be served with nachos, tortillas, lettuce, and/or rice.

It tastes like a boiled mix of blood and flesh. It does not taste like it was made by someone with gravitas and determination but rather like someone enduring a persistent mental illness that clings tightly. It is akin to the taste of Jodorowsky's *Santa Sangre*. It resembles the taste of feijoada, which slaves in Brazil created by boiling red beans and discarded pig ears from butchers. It tastes like the novel Zorg will finish writing after dressing as a woman and suffocating Betty with a pillow. This taste seems to affirm that blood is an ingredient of the sun.

THE PAST NOT YET HERE

Tomorrow is gone.
Yesterday will arrive.

Death was born.
Birth is far.

LIFE OF A STAGE DIRECTOR

This is a profile of a stage director I meet sometimes:
He drew the attention of theater critics.
He was surrounded by friends of the opposite sex.
He drew the attention of theater critics.
He got married.
He drew the attention of theater critics.
He sold his house to produce a play.
He took out the mortgage to produce a play.
He got divorced.
He drew the attention of theater critics.
He became unemployed.
He grew a beard.
He was a raggedy man.
He became a mean drunk.
He couldn't control his temper.
The theater critics were silent.

ESCAPING

Because they still think of themselves as the standard by which all creation is measured, some people grow angry when confronted with the unfamiliar.

They use the power of the self to condemn the other. Such people are especially quick to anger when confronted with poetry, created from that all-too-common tool known as language.

There may be an escape that ruins both body and mind, driven by an extraordinary way of thinking about poetry.

For instance, writing difficult poetry.

An escape in which one who despises being fully understood ends up losing oneself within the text.

An escape toward death, toward avoiding understanding, rather than the time spent getting torn apart so as to be fully understood.

The sacrifice of becoming a profound monster, subject to random stop-and-frisk by Aerok readers,

Or enduring the monster's ennui for a lifetime.

For months, I've had a poem taped to the bathroom door and have been reading it.

Every time I read it, the poem points toward another direction, toward another world.

RENÉ MAGRITTE AND THE CHARLES BONNET SYNDROME

At the Beyer Art Museum in Basel, I attended the René Magritte exhibition.

After viewing his works, I felt that René Magritte, who only used his house and childhood memories as the subjects of his paintings, must have been experiencing Charles Bonnet syndrome. This condition causes individuals to see everyday objects, like a pebble on a table,

grow larger like a planet veering off its orbit, advancing relentlessly toward their eyes. A patient paralyzed from that fear. An artist, documenting it with chilling precision.

His paintings lay on the boundary between patient and artist.

His mother, a hat seller, ended her life by jumping from a roof, and for the rest of his life, Magritte never let go of the skirt of his wife, Josette. (He did not, however, continually depict his wife's back, as we know Hammershøi did.)

A wife's lace, a mackerel for supper, a personal smoking pipe,
A remaining bottle of wine, an unripe apple or one with a leaf, a dining chair, a pocket key,
A doorknob, a table bell, the sky through a window,
Clouds engulfing each dish,
And clouds squeezing through every crevice, these trivial items,

He rendered them unfamiliar. The grand became minute, and the minute expanded, as in *Gulliver's Travels*,

Placing objects in the sky, embedding them in spaces of illusion, metaphorizing, automatic drawing, metonymy, association, altering the positions of shadow and its source, interchanging being and non-being, projecting rhetoric onto objects.

Lady No returns to her riverside lodging, and

My two eyes,
My two ears,
My two hands,
My two feet,
My two nipples,

My ears long to gaze upon each other, thus they depart from my body and take flight tonight.

A comb, larger than a bed, rests upon it.
A soap brush, surpassing a cupboard in size, sits atop one.

A wine glass, dwarfing the room, stands on a carpet.
A white moon, perfectly fitting within the glass.

Charles Bonnet visited Lady No.

TO NOT ROT AFTER DEATH

To be mummified alive, to be a floating corpse, this is what you must do. First, boil grain. Next, climb mountains. The mountains should be clean and fresh, covered in snow. Then, walk. Walk again. Walk all day. Only eat nuts. After a while, stop eating them, too. Subsist only on resin and the barks of pine trees. They will be your preservatives. Your fingernails will grow thin. The muscles inside your eardrums will soften and you will hear as clearly as is imaginable. You will hear a mosquito from leagues away. Your organs will shrink. Your stomach will shrink so much that a single walnut will be difficult to digest. Without this hard labor, the fat of your body will absorb the water of your body as you starve to death. Too much water will rot your body. The dead body rots when it absorbs water. You must also reduce how much you drink. Endure only with the strength of your muscles and organs. Your body will be so light that when you try to take a bath it will float on water. Someone will have to press you down so that your body will sink into the tub. There won't be pain. It will be tiring, and your stomach will prickle now and then. You will meditate. Meditation will serve to stop your metabolism. You will drink tea made from the red sap of poison ivy. Because you won't have the flesh of your skin for the ivy's poison to swell in, the color of the ivy will seep into your stomach and intestines. Enjoy bathing in hot springs until breath leaves your body. Hot springs filled with arsenic are preferred. That will kill the germs, bacteria, and potential maggots. All the pink inside your body will be killed. After many years of this process, taken step by step, you will become a completely dried-out mummy, and the breath of your life will slip out of your body. You will be sitting upright when you die. No one will know. You will be so light that you won't return to earth.

Your body will be preserved for centuries and millennia. You will be a tourist attraction. You will even be worshipped.

AEROK FICTION FACTORY

There once was a country where beatings produced works of fiction.

The tools needed for producing such fictions were clubs, screams, and bathtubs.

There were various methods of completing a work of fiction, such as beating, hanging, and pushing a writer's face into water.

When a writer's progress on their fiction slowed down, the screaming of friends, relatives, parents, and spouses were brought into the adjoining room, and this pushed the peak of the fiction's climax higher.

The employees of the Fiction Factory only needed to repeat this one order: Confess! Confess! Confess!

These encouragements to create fiction did not stop until it was possible for the writers to say "I didn't do it," or "I did it."

Aerok Fiction Factory was a booming business.

After the fiction writing was over, fiction writers were cast out

To some seashore or to some mountain valley in such secret

That not even the sewer rats knew what had happened.

Or they were thrown into solitary cells for decades

And the only way to reduce their sentence was by raising the shock value of their fiction.

Fiction Writer H came home from the Fiction Factory and their body was the color of ink

And they suffered aphasia for months.

After ages passed, such fictions were completed, fictions no one would ever want to read again.

However, we come from those fiction factories.

We were born there.

Some time ago, right before one of those fiction factories could be renovated into an art museum, I went down to its third basement floor

And there were the fiction writers, who had become ghosts, unable to leave the haunted hallways,

And their mumblings would not cease, their minds utterly lost in the writing of their fictions.

After ages passed, when the daily recordkeeper of Aerok's tortures was elected mayor,

an order came down that now instead of beatings, carrots would be hung around everyone's neck.

THE NAME OF POETRY

The country of poetry is where a name is erased.

A place where I can say, "I am the secretary of an invisible girl. I simply transcribe what she dictates."

A poet who came to speak to me said, "Please call your own name, then draw your future and tell us about it."

The poetry of 'I' is where the name of 'I' is erased.
There, 'I' is the one who is most terrified of the name of 'I.'
Poetry is the language of the one who has fallen beneath one's name.
Because one's name carries death.
Because in poetry 'my' is the one who can't stand 'I' the most.
Once one has run far away from a name, poetry finally begins.

Poetry goes beyond a 'name,' beyond identity, toward the pattern I drew as I was washed out into anonymity. The design of that pattern. Where verbs and adjectives try to fulfill themselves by drawing patterns inside the design, where pronouns and nouns turn into verbs and scatter. It is the secret of their escape.

A nameless one
A nameless one, s/he whose name no one knows in the world,
The one whose name everyone else has forgotten
Is coming down the valley.
S/he kisses the stream of the valley and drinks its water.
The blue sky clings to his/her sleeves.

INSIDE OF WINNING

The season of college entrance exams was upon us. The admission ratio was crushing. A current student at the college came to my office and reenacted the day he had received his acceptance letter. "I texted my father my name alongside the name of the college and my class year," he told me. "My father called me back in tears," he told me. The student defined those days after his acceptance to the college as the days of barbeques and gifts. Now, he is the future that the current crop of applicants are dreaming of. The banality, the boredom, and the disappointment he now experiences is the inside of winning for someone who has never won. This is probably how the days of our lives are. Who could've known that the insides of our lives, which have survived this far by pushing off someone else's, would be trembling with so much loneliness, boredom, and anxiety?

CUTE GRANDPA

She watches a cute old man in a subway car.
A cute old man standing in front of the car's doors.
A short, cute old man.
Lady No likes to observe such cute grandpas.
This old man is wearing a cute fur hat, perhaps a gift from Inuits.
If someone bigger had worn it, that someone might have looked like a KGB agent,
But since it is a cute old man wearing it the hat looks like a theater prop.
This old man doesn't like to sit in the seats reserved for the elderly and disabled.
He is always wearing cute sneakers that are too big for him and stands next to the doors.
This old man's eyes are small, and his face and hands are wrinkly.
But sir, where are you going, why don't you sit here—
He smiles when he hears this, cute dimples forming on his cheeks.
Lady No wants to see those dimples again and again
So she keeps yielding her seat to him.
The cute old man doesn't grow any older, but neither does he become more solemn.
This is because the 'cute' wells up from his body.
When the old man gets on a subway car, the whole car turns cute.

Lady No writes in her notebook, "the word 'cute' exists in this world."
She writes her hope for all men to be cuter.

THE LIPS OF THE SONGS

A radio sits alone in an open meadow.

It has a battery larger than its body and plays many songs, with its owner nowhere in sight.

The songs are foreign, their lyrics enigmatic, yet the lips of the songs kiss the lips of the clouds.

The songs are as tough as threads crafted from delicate winds.

The songs persist, reminiscent of relentless swarms of flies circling over vomit.

I search in every direction, but it appears no one is approaching to turn the radio off.

In my childhood, I visited the home of my maternal family, where no one lives now.

That was the place where a laundry line, stretched taut by some hand, stood alone.

There, I tried to rouse my grandpa, who lay beneath a utility pole along a major highway after vomiting one morning,

Alone until I stood motionless by his side.

A pitiful little radio is like the child I was back then,

Broadcasting only to itself and listening only to itself in this vast world.

Suddenly, slender fingers emerge from the soil. Can this be real?

The songs, dipping their fingers into the cold wind for a taste, retreat swiftly, startled.

The songs like the winds that the vast meadow attempts to embrace over and over.

From afar, a shepherd
Hastens with a black dog, while
The boundless meadow quietly listens to the songs of the radio.

FICTION AND POETRY

To write fiction is to record that life is a marvelous lie.

Recording in advance that after you and I disappear, only faint lies will remain, growing even fainter.

Thus, recording in advance the sight of lies, on a street without 'I,' being swept away by other lies.

To write poetry is to witness my death in poetry.

The apex of poetry is the moment of death, the moment when only death remains in the shape of a mustard seed and all else becomes absence.

Thus, the act of writing a poem now means to endure while embracing a firefly-like death with a gentle breath.

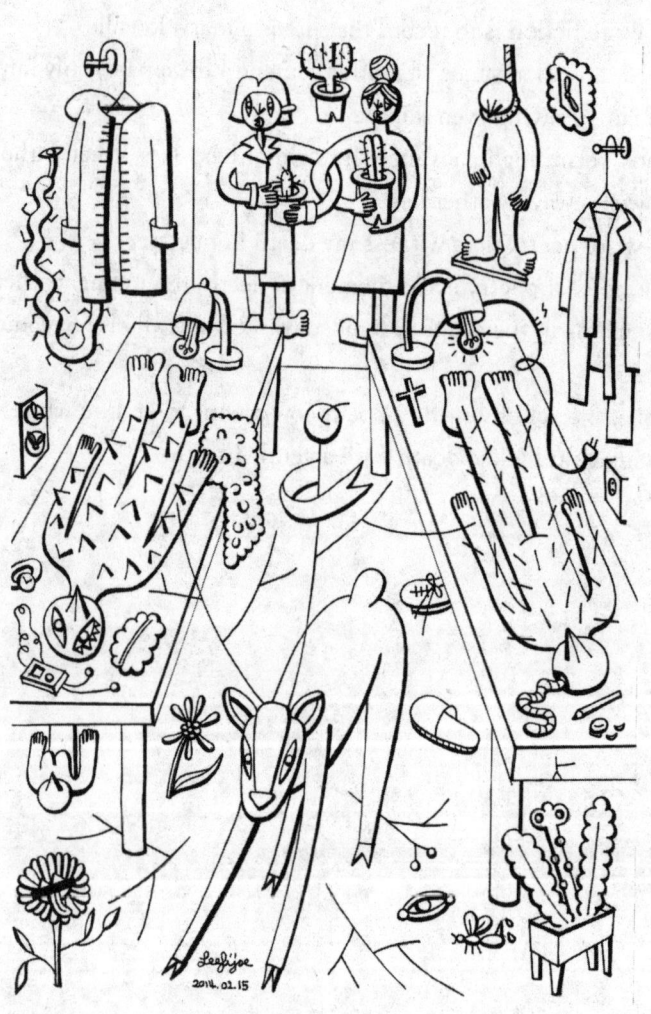

OUT-OF-DATE GENRES

An order was issued.

Poetry and fiction are now out-of-date genres.

Poetry and fiction have fulfilled their duties for the ages and are now relieved.

Therefore, they should provide stories to digital media platforms.

Please stop circling the edge of politics, economics, sociology, and culture, and become workers of industry and take on more constructive roles.

Give poetry to ads, narratives to video games, and plots to comics.

Draw rough sketches for TV shows, come up with dialogue for movies, and

Why don't you write stories that can be used as outlines for musicals?

An order was issued.

Like mushrooms blossoming after rain, many new courses are being introduced:

Television and Digital Media Storytelling,

Film and Digital Media Storytelling,

Comics and Digital Media Storytelling,

Publishing and Digital Media Storytelling,

Fiction and Digital Media Storytelling.

All around the country, many university departments have changed their names to Digital Media Creative Writing or Digital Media Literary Fine Arts or Digital Media Storytelling Creative Writing.

Included in every course description and title are English words like "new media contents."

Students who have just graduated from high schools, who have never taken a course in mythologies or histories or any kind of humanities,

Are now being mobilized for the development of new digital media storytelling contents.

They must discard out-of-date genres and become creators of digital media.

How can the genre of poetry contribute to digital media storytelling?

As I charge into the classroom with my attendance book, I carefully think about it.

Kim Soo-young and Kim Chu-su and Digital Media Contents Storytelling!

And all you dedicated creators of digital media content!

THE PRIVILEGE OF BLEEDING

A child who had been humiliated by her friend spoke to Lady No.
Please take me to a hospital.
But Lady No told the child to go back and take revenge.
And the child said,
I am bleeding inside my head. Please take me to a hospital.
Everyone bleeds inside their heads! answered Lady No.
Underneath pure white quilt between pure white walls,
Exercising the privilege of bleeding,
A child lay still, wanting to take revenge against her friend, and lying beside the child
Lady No imagined a revenge that dug into the grave's embrace.
She imagined taking revenge and exercising the privilege of disappearing forever.
Lady No asked the child.
Whatcha doin'?
Imagining.
Me too.

SEEING THE MULTI-GENRE AUDIENCE

I went to a movie theater in Rajasthan.

There were six of us.

We wore skirts and heels, covered ourselves in shawls, and ironed our pants because we wanted to look good at the movies.

The movie we watched was a multi-genre piece: noir-melo-action-adventure-horror-thriller-musical.

We laughed our heads off as an entire life unfolded before us.

But then we saw the other members of the audience and we were shocked.

Except for us, they were all men.

The men cried, laughed, shouted, and lamented.

Over the next two hours, we had a complete collection of joy, anger, sorrow, and pleasure.

When everyone moaned the same way at the same time, it was a sight to behold.

Soon, it became more fun for us to observe the audience than the movie.

We got more and more into the audience.

If you visit Rajasthan, I recommend seeing the multi-genre audience instead of a Bollywood movie.

PAYING RESPECT TO THE FOOD

The old movie *Tampopo* shows us how to eat Japanese noodles.

First, you must pay respect to the dish.
You must appreciate its shape and smell its essential fragrance.

Then, you must pay respect to how the food has come together in harmony.
You must appreciate the jewel-like shining of the oil spots upon the broth.
You must take pleasure in the fragrance of floating scallions.
You must pay respect to the three pieces of sliced boiled pork.
The pork that was central to the noodle but is now humble in its form.
You must pay respect to its fallen form.
Steam rises slowly.
You must pay respect to the steam as well.

Then, you must pay respect to the food itself.
You must gently pat the surface of the noodle.
You must especially pat the slices of pork.
Then, you must dip the pork into the broth.
(And then you must apologize to the pork with utmost sincerity.
You must entreat it with formal language and say, "I'll see you soon, sir," and then pray.)
You must eat the noodles first.
You must pay respect by slurping them loudly.
As you slurp the noodles, you must not forget to occasionally give loving glances to the pork slices.

The final respect to pay is respect to the broth.
You must drink it three times while sighing each time.

You must shake off the liquid from the pork slices as if making an important decision.

You must mutter repeatedly, "I'm sorry and I'm grateful," while doing so.

I eat the fear of the things that came to me and became what I consume.

Their fears have become my anxieties, probably.

I think about the things that became my hours, and about their screams and fears and anxieties.

I think about my superficial life, keeping its mouth shut, pushing them deep down.

LAST OUNCE OF STRENGTH

Sherpas are climbing up the Himalayas.
An entire family, wearing ropes around their heads,
with luggage bigger than their bodies attached to those ropes, is climbing.
Climbing precariously up the cliff edge.
It is raining, and they are climbing to the place from which the rain falls.
In the rain, sweat pours down like rainfall, and urine flows uncontrollably.
Do not praise worker ants for their diligence; they are slaves.
The queen below earth hatches their deaths.
Not one of them opens their mouths to speak, so do not push your camera lenses to their faces.
They have no time to speak. Their shining eyes do nothing but climb.
A woman, hiding her skinny legs in her skirt,
carries twelve bottles of fresh water while climbing the Himalayas.
Her eyeballs are sweating, and her nails spew sweat.
She is climbing only so that she can put them down.
Like groundwater painstakingly drawn up from deep underground,
only to be powerfully discarded into the bathtub of a mountaintop resort,
she climbs, ready to cast herself away with the same wild abandon.
When the sun sets underneath her feet, a sour taste climbs up from all the way below.

Like climbing back up a path inside one's body through which milk flows,
    like crawling back into the holes where sweat fills up,
    like climbing back through the way where shit gets tangled up,
    like baby swallows chirping with their red beaks wide open, like a mother swallow who hears nothing but that sound,
    She
    Is
    Climbing
    Up.

APRIL

ARCTIC

An iceberg appeared, and as she approached, it became whiter and grander. The iceberg was almost blue. Once she was right next to it, the iceberg revealed itself to be entirely made of A4-sized papers. These white papers were filled with words written in blue ink, but the words were melting in water, making them impossible to read. They were poems Lady No had written all her life. Some poems were bound, some were crumpled, and others were spilling out. Who could have possibly brought them here? The poems were turning into ice. A ship was buried inside the iceberg. The white papers scattered in the wind. Sometimes, an Arctic seagull, made of white papers, suddenly rose out from it all.

LADY NO'S FRANCE

French people aren't dead, but people say France is in a museum.
They say she is in antique art stores.

France is in America, as well as in Aerok.
France came all the way here?
France is sold at an auction.

France was on the wall of my mother's living room, gently lighting her house.
France is now so common in the world that it is impossible to call France France.
France is as common as a painting of a girl in the sunshine.
France rolls around on a shelf because she can't even be trashed.
France can't even be called grandma, or even an ancestral matriarch.
Why did the people of the world pin France on the wall?
France is submerged in the delicate smoke or in the wine's evaporation.
Let's go sailing, O Albatross! O you who belong to short White people!
France must be let go along with the family's secrets.
Why do all bygone secrets become mediocre paintings?

Near the back gate of my college, there is a restaurant called France, and they sell French wine and French food,
but it has lost customers, and when you go there now
France gets more uncomfortable with the person sitting alone in the empty hall.

They say French people do not read poetry from other countries, and they don't even read poetry from their own.

France is in my family's house,
I do not get taxed even though I have France.
But now, I want to throw out France and move to a nice clean house.

Still, Lady No thinks. France that is within me helped me endure.
Using a place that was positioned on the opposite side of Lady No, it helped Lady No to love her house.

Because of France, Lady No could even endure a little bit of herself.

A WRITING SCRIPT ONLY WOMEN USE

A baby-footed woman wrote a letter to another baby-footed woman.
"I fear the man at night. The man's mother beat me. It's a shame the flowers are falling. I want to see you."

Upon receiving this letter, the other baby-footed woman wrote her reply.
"My body hurts. I lie down from pain, but the man's mother won't give me food. The man is older than my father. My twisted feet are rotting. My younger sister with big feet got sold into slavery.
I want to see you."

Once, there was a country where women had a writing script only for themselves.
Men could neither read nor use it.

A bigger country invaded and burned all the writings women had written.
I bought a pillowcase with pink silk embroidery that formed a few of their words. I hugged it like I would baby's feet. I want to write letters with those women's scripts. I want to build a house of writing.

THE WORST SHAME IN LIFE

It is a film about shame.

The camera rarely ventures outside the house.
Perhaps walking through a flooded hallway in a dream was the only time one could leave the house.

Shame is a sensation that pushes us to wish for eternal disappearance.

On a certain floor of an apartment building, there lived two elderly individuals.
One of them collapsed.
And
Lady No does not wish to document what followed.
It is too heavy for a heart to endure.

Aging is shameful.
Falling ill is shameful.
Moreover, how shameful 'dying' is.

When the time arrives when shame can no longer be felt,
If only there was someone beside them who could erase him/her from the world.

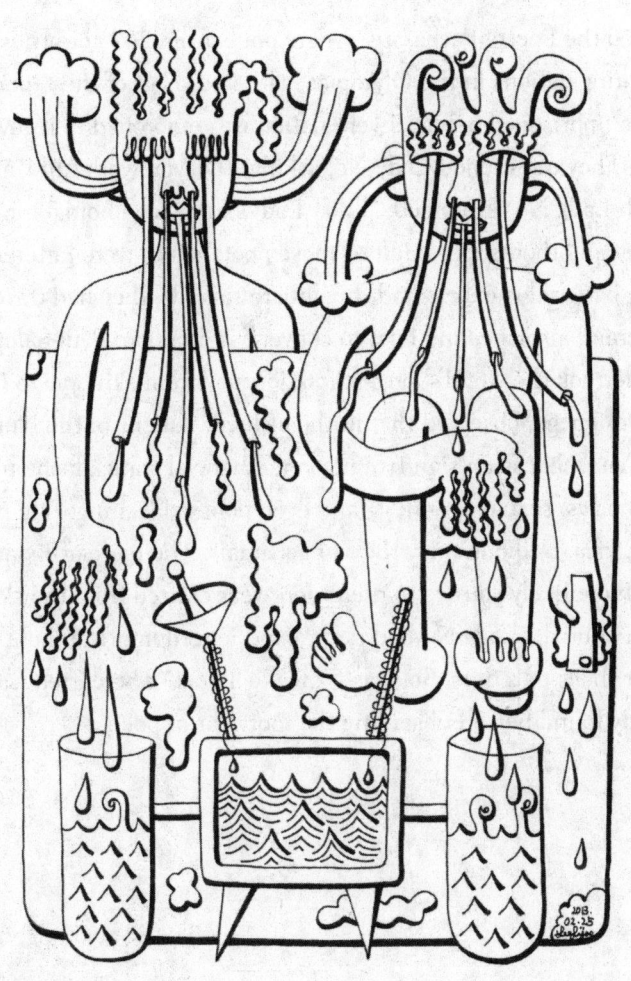

THUS SPOKE LADY NO

I attended the Poetry Parnassus, where poets from 202 countries, all participating nations in the Olympics, gathered. Half of these poets had been imprisoned before. Every nation was embroiled in its own conflict. They questioned Lady No, asking, "Do you work full-time?" To which Lady No responded, "I do." Lady No took a photograph of each poet and their shoes. Half of these poets' shoes were tattered. Wearing battered sneakers and threadbare sandals, they had traveled by bus, train, airplane, and boat to convene in London. Paul Salopek, who undertook the world's longest foot journey from Ethiopia to Chile's Tierra Del Fuego, observed that in the affluent nations of the Northern Hemisphere, shoes can signify a person's financial status, fashion sense, career choices, sexual openness, and even political leanings. He noted that in Africa, millions sport the same sandals. The more affluent you are, the more likely you are to prefer footwear crafted from the skin of newborn animals. Lady No had never experienced imprisonment nor worn her shoes to tatters. So, was Lady No a poet? Thereafter, Lady No frequently found herself observing the footwear of poets.

NO WORDS TO EXPRESS THE BODY

The ground clings to Lady No only as much as her shoes. Surrounded by cliffs on all sides.

Each time Lady No moves forward, the ground follows and clings only as much as her shoes.

Lady No imagines larger shoes for herself. Then she would be less dizzy.

Shoes the size of a football field. Shoes the size of my country.

Doctors at various hospitals have asked Lady No,
Does the sky spin? Does your body spin? Does the ground rise? Is the ground like a sponge?
Does the road ascend when you drive?
Does it feel like you are on a spinning turntable?
Do you feel seasick?
Do the words spin, do your eyes spin?
Does it feel like you are falling?
Do objects tremble?
Do you feel like your head is floating?
Do you vomit?
Is it dark?
In front of each doctor's desk, Lady No struggled to articulate her dizziness. Suddenly, Lady No envisioned a scene of objects falling like three thousand ladies of the royal palace. They were snow people. Not the snowmen you build with children in the shape of an 8, but real snow people. White as snow, malleable as snow, blanketing our final moments like snow, as small as white mice emerging from human noses, these snow beings kept falling.

Lady No couldn't share these thoughts with the doctor. She couldn't find an appropriate adjective.

Thus spoke Lady No: My fingertips are teetering-teetering, my arms are teetering-teetering, my thighs are teetering-teetering, my chest is teetering-teetering, my stomach is teetering-teetering.

And then, the doctor responded,
You are experiencing vertigo.

Words are never enough to describe the body.

ROGER CORMAN

The TV was broadcasting an old Aerok film, so I decided to watch it with my daughter,
    the kind of movie that could suddenly flood our eyes with tears.
    The main character recited a poem by our country's most famous poet.
    The poem was about waiting and having faith that the snow will stop, the flowers will blossom, the leaves will fall, and that the snow will pour down again.

    I remembered hearing that after the poem was recited in the film, the volume in which the poem was collected sold tens of thousands more copies.
    Thus spoke Lady No:
    "I hope one of my poems will be recited in a movie so that my books will sell well, too."
    Then, the daughter of Lady No recited some titles of movies that could have worked with poems of Lady No:

House of Usher
Deep-Sea Monster
Cry Baby Killer
The Wild Angels
Attack of the Crab Monsters
Dinoshark
Killer Monster
Croc

They were the titles of movies by Roger Corman.

BARELY LIGHT BARELY WHITE BARELY RIGHT

The camera and the screen have become the dealers of direct experience. Experiences that one had to interpret for oneself every day seem to have evaporated and are no more.

This semester, the students were given an assignment titled 'Barely Light, Barely White, Barely Right.'

For example, after their day was over, they were tasked with writing down how events and landscapes passed them by during the day, barely light.

How the language of poetry, after hiding in twilight, rides out on the air we breathe, creating flickering flashes, and how the light breathes barely light, staying in motion while riding the language of poetry.

How a gesture, on which it seemed a wandering soul was laid to rest, is nowhere to be found.

How the landscape of the afterlife, barely white in the mind, may seem.

How, before emerging in language, after rising from being submerged under the inner landscapes, the past must go through certain mechanisms before it reappears, and how some of it ends up appearing and some of it remains hidden.

How the light that was moaning earns the first body of language, that pinkish naked body, at a certain moment, but how the more of it is laid on top of language, the more it becomes obscured.

How the shape of language, before its awakening, before it was divided into image, meaning, and sound, may have seemed (was it like ectoplasm, was it like snot).

One looks at twilight, thinking it is beautiful because it has no path, no body, no answer.

Dim is the gesture entering this evening's words. If there is a perfume one sprays on oneself when one breaks up with the world, then the gesture is as obfuscated as that perfume settling in. The gesture is as obscure as the motions the dead left behind while they lived.

The ghost's barely light.
The silence's barely light.
The naked body's barely light.

Tonight, Lady No's dream casts a barely light on Lady No's brain.

EMERGENCY ROOM

A small cat appeared in her stomach.

At first, it was the size of a mosquito, but soon it grew to the size of a mouse.

Waking from her sleep, Lady No opened her eyes wide.

She looked at the clock.

Everyone was asleep at this hour.

In a hot minute, the cat grew bigger.

Finally, a mother cat appeared in her stomach.

Holding her stomach, Lady No writhed.

And then, the emergency room.

People there thought very little of Lady No, who had a stomach full of cats.

They yelled at her to stop screaming.

The emergency room was crowded with patients who could not be admitted.

Endless sounds of wheels, endless sounds of fighting.

The ECG operator, with sleepy eyes, ordered her to lie down straight, even though she couldn't.

They told her to keep walking through different rooms, even though she couldn't.

Many photographs of the cat, Lady No's insides, were taken.

And while waiting for the results, a nurse ordered her to go out and sit in the chair for visitors because there were no more beds.

Lady No memorized the nurse's name. "You wait and see, Nurse YBR!"

She chewed on the name between her moans.

Unable to lie down or sit, holding an awkward pose, she stared at a neon sign that spelled "Emergency Room" for four hours.

The pain was in the shape of a beast. It had its own life separate from Lady No.

Lady No was summoned by YBR.

When the morning came, the pain lessened along with the dark.

AVANT-GARDE POET

She went to read her poems.
The moderator asked her.
How were you able to practice avant-garde for so long?
Lady No answered.
For so long, all I did was keep saying to myself, 'This isn't it, this isn't it.'
And at some point, if it wasn't, 'This isn't it,' then it didn't feel like a poem.
She added, Whenever I felt I had written a poem about which I could say, 'This is it,' I threw it away.

If I am really an avant-garde poet like you just said, then please keep calling me one! O please, Mister Critic Moderator. That sounds so cool!

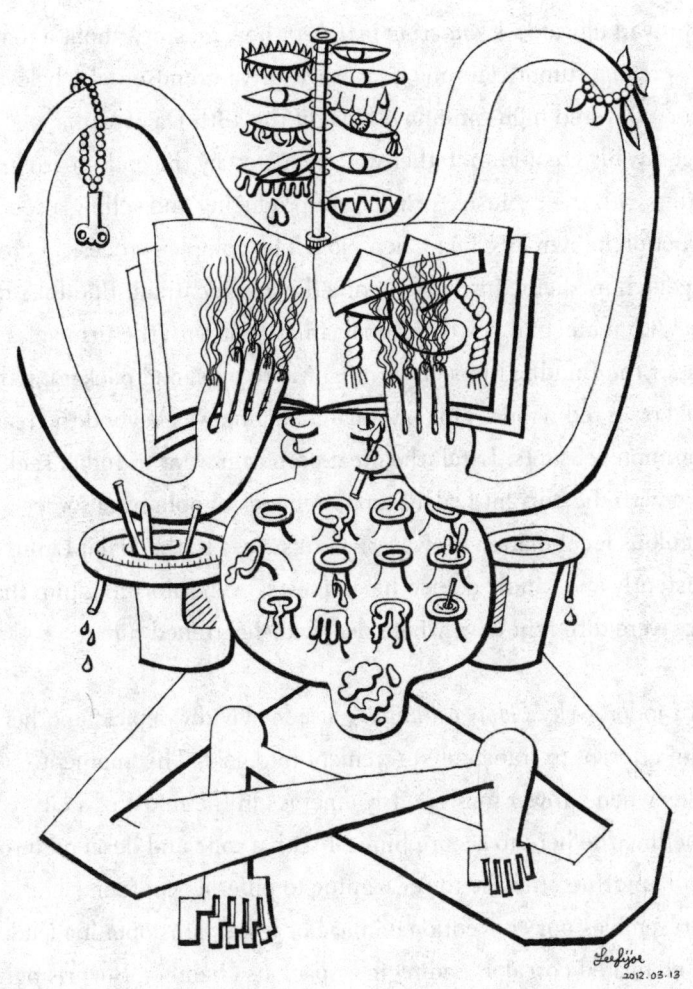

POOP

In Shinya Fujiwara's *Wandering in Tibet*, there's a story about a man who spread a rumor claiming he was the great-grandson of a beloved doctor, a favored high-ranking official of the 13th Dalai Lama. Allegedly, his great-grandfather was entrusted by the god-incarnate Buddha with the exclusive privilege of producing and selling a secret concoction known as Chua Chen Nolf. The complex process of creating this golden medicine involved mixing the god-incarnate Buddha's dried feces with medicinal powders, amalgamating it with the urine of a high priest or the Buddha himself, forming it into pills, and packaging these in gold or in red wraps. This mystical medicine was beyond the reach of common peasants. Later, the great-grandson went to India, seeking refuge with the current Dalai Lama, in hopes of obtaining some miraculous fecal matter. However, monks close to the Dalai Lama consistently and kindly denied his requests, even informing him that things were different now, which deeply disheartened him.

In Jodorowsky's *Holy Mountain*, a scene vividly depicts another fervent attempt to transmute excrement into gold. This moment unfolds when a tower mysteriously emerges in the midst of a city, compelling the hero to secure himself with a rope and descend into a small aperture atop the tower, aiming to pilfer its contents. The hero resembles our conventional image of Jesus. This opening leads to an elongated corridor, ending in a spacious chamber. Surprisingly, this chamber fits within a geometric structure, where the alchemist Jodorowsky awaits. He rises slowly, as if anticipating the Messiah's arrival, feigning a welcome before forcefully casting Jesus to the ground. The method by which he violates the hero's intestines remains ambiguous, yet he collects the hero's feces in a clear bowl and undertakes an alchemical process to transform it into gold.

That just goes to show how incredible our organs really are. That just goes to show how we consume and excrete substances derived from the earth, sea, and air, and how we might be excreting things that could one day turn into gold. So, could we not imagine that the excretions of figures like the Dalai Lama or Jesus are distinct from our own, possessing the miraculous ability to be converted into extraordinary medicines, we could?

SENTENCE ENDINGS FOR FATHERS AND MEN

Fathers' sentences always end with 'don't' (마라).
Don't eat the fruit.
Don't steal.
Don't have affairs.
Don't go to heaven.

Men's sentences always end with 'please give' (다오).
Please give me your breasts.
Please give me your pink lips.
Please give me your thighs.
I will give you heaven.

But there is similarity between 'don't' and 'please give'.
Don't open the door, you will die if you do. (fathers)
Please open the door, I will please you to death you if you do. (misters)
You die anyway.

DOCUMENT HUMAN

I was late.
Please submit a written document.
I cannot attend.
Please submit a written document.
I am currently unable to submit paperwork.
Please submit a written document.
I want to see a concert.
Please submit a written document.
That person is defaming me.
Please submit a written document.
I think I need to go to the ER.
Please submit a written document.
I am not that kind of person.
Please submit a written document.
Does the administration only ever ask for documents?
Please submit a written document.
I am dying right now.
Please submit a written document.

If Lady No doesn't complete and submit her documents, she was told, her students will risk losing their tuition loans and subsequent funding. Consequently, she must complete this document. Despite her objections to the document, she must complete it with positivity. She must complete it while keeping her mouth closed. She must complete it, bleeding pink through her nose. She must produce writing that she doesn't know how it will be used. She must inscribe words on flags that will be used only once and then thrown into trash cans. She must raise such a flag and move forward.

MOZART

After watching Larry Weinstein's *Mozartballs*

Mozart died and became a woman.
After becoming a woman, Mozart fell in love with a woman who became Constanze after Constanze had died.
Whenever Mozart embraced Constanze, he begged her to piss on his face.

Mozart died and became an astronaut's bathwater.
The astronaut was fully submerged in Mozart, who filled the bathtub of his spaceship.
And the astronaut watched as his wife on Earth gave birth to their daughter.
After taking his bath, the astronaut was thrown down to the bottom of the universe.

Mozart died and became his self-cloner.
Once Mozart was entered into the computer, Mozarts of numerous possibilities came pouring out.
Mozarts of tens of thousands of mutations all claimed that they were Mozart.
When I came to my senses and slapped one of those Mozarts,
Every Mozart screamed Ahk! and held their cheeks.

Mozart died and became a worshipper at the grave of Mozart.
The worshipper rubbed his lips on his grave every day and mumbled.
O Mozart's pink lips, come out of the grave and
Receive these rough lips of ugly and old Mozart!

Mozart died and became a Choco Ball.

Every day five thousand Choco Mozarts were hatched on a conveyor belt.

I peeled off Mozart's silver wig and sucked his sweet head whole.

Fresh yellow Mozart juice is dripping

One drop at a time on my head this morning, heavier and brighter than a drop of Earth.

I thought about the grave issue of Mr. Mozart's rate of reproduction.

More Mozarts were pouring out than what two crazy rats could produce in ten years,

And now they were filling up my room this morning.

All was composed, and I was all played out.

LIVING FICTION

On the last day of the semester, a face rose from memory. It was the face of a student, wearing a large hat like Princess Diana, dressed in a sundress with pink flower patterns. She was older than most of the other students.

This student always said that only direct experience could be the ingredients of fiction, and that she would only write fiction based on what she experienced. I thought she might change her mind after taking some classes and graduating.

One day, the student wrote a piece of fiction. It was about the death of a heroine who lived through the Gwangju Uprising.

After she finished writing her long fiction, she disappeared.

When the teaching assistant went to the student's residence after repeated attempts at contacting her had failed,

It was discovered that she had already departed for the next world of her own accord.

She had written in her journals that she was an orphan and that she was a victim of the uprising.

Because she insisted that all her fiction was based on direct experiences, the teacher of her fiction writing class said that if her fiction were investigated, perhaps some evidence about what happened to her could be found.

According to her fiction, she had no family or friends.

All she had was the revolution. All she had was post-traumatic disorder following the failure of the revolution.

Out of options, the teachers from her department decided to give her a funeral.

But after reaching out to many different places,

Her family appeared. Her parents were still alive, and she had many siblings.

She had not lived like the plot of her fiction, but she had departed like the end of her fiction. Lady No actually thinks of her often.

When she does, it is always as if a slight terror has passed by,

So pale that they are sticky with blueness—the face beneath her hat, and her bottomless gentle voice.

THE DESK CLOCK IN THE MAIN BUDDHA HALL

Hélène and Lady No toured the Buddhist temples of Southeastern Aerok. The dark temples, covered in fallen leaves, hushed.
Hélène asked Lady No,
"In your country's temples, in front of the largest Buddhas in the temple's main halls, why is there always a pink lotus blossom with a desk clock? The clocks look out of place in thousand-year-old temples."
At Bongjeong Temple, Lady No finally asked a monk about this.
The monk pulled up his sleeves to show his wrist and answered,
"We do not own wristwatches.
But we must start and end our worship at appointed times."
Lady No explained this to Hélène, but Hélène asked another question,
"Wouldn't it be better to own a wristwatch?"

A DIALOGUE FROM APICHATPONG WEERASETHAKUL'S FILM *SYNDROMES AND A CENTURY*

(Even though they couldn't remember every line of dialogue,
 a friend who had watched the film with her told Lady No that she would now perform a psych test on her.)

Among a triangle, a square, and a circle, which would you choose?
Circle.
If you were to draw a circle, how big and what color would it be?
Transparent glass.
(Saying, 'I don't remember the rest.')
What will you make with the glass?
A glass cup.
What will you put in it?
Lady No's pink blood.
What will you do with that liquid?
Pour it on the ground.
Ants will eat it.
There is a bag.
What's in the bag?
Meat.
What kind of meat is it?
Lean.
Form an image in your mind.
You are walking through a forest.
There is a great waterfall and

a flowing stream.
Something is floating on the stream.
What is it?
A corpse.

I think you are going to need a full psych eval, the friend said.

A MESSAGE FROM LADY NO

Hello,
These days weigh heavy on our hearts.
We would like to relay the message from Lady No that she will be taking time off from her serialization for a few weeks.
We ask for your generous understanding and hope you will continue to have interest in Lady No and Fi Jae Lee's blog series when they return.

MAY

DRIZZLING APRIL

No one in Aerok can sleep.

They pretend to be asleep though they are awake.

In houses with the lights turned off, people are awake. People are in their beds with their eyes open.

None of them want the others to know they are awake. They all pretend to be asleep.

It is drizzling.

A bird's nest on a tree is completely drenched.

Pink cherry blossom leaves wither like thin fingernails that clawed into air.

The beach is so drenched that it is getting heavy.

Someone stands outside the door.

They are drenched.

They will disappear when we open our eyes.

They cannot be embraced because they are like vapor.

They are as pitiful as haze.

A shadow wobbles upon the window.

They have come for us.

A perfectly fitting frame for us.

A mold made from the frame of tears taken from our bodies.

It is drizzling.

Our eyes are opening.

METAPHOR BAN

Metaphor has been stolen from the poet.
The ocean is no longer a place of metaphor.
Lady No once metaphorized in a poem that she was entering water.
Tying a ribbon of metaphor on the vast world.
Forgiveness must be sought for these acts.

Seasons have been stolen from the poet.
After spring, summer does not follow. It is hot winter.
Flowers blossom all at once then die all at once.
Lady No, who once described a bud of a flower as like a tightly held fist
As a metaphor in a poem, must seek forgiveness.

God's now been stolen from Lady No.
It is now difficult to pray to God.

For the chirping songs of baby chicks, forgiveness must be sought.
This spring, the chicks got stuck on fences.
They hang from people's chests and sleeves.

Black rain raining on stolen spring.
From the eaves, pink flesh of stolen God
Splattering down down down.
I can't even bring myself to call it a stolen sea, metaphorically.

Is there any metaphor in this country now.

Perhaps if we are forgiven
Perhaps if every poem in this world is forgiven.

EASTER

    Lady No wears funeral clothes and goes to work in the city.
    When the train is near the destination,
    Passengers are told to step off the train at the next station for shuttle bus transfer, and
    Passengers who are going on foot are to step off the train at the station after next.
    Can you believe there's a country where subway announcements direct you to funeral halls?

    After the class is over, we go to pay our respects.
    At the end of a long line, we bow our heads and offer chrysanthemums.
    As the long line gets shorter, fresh, clean, clear,
    and vivid faces dangle from the pit of our stomachs.

    Mourners are quiet. They've come from far away.
    Despite the long wait, only a few complain.
    After offering their flowers and taking a moment of silence, they all cry.
    When they come out, mourners are given tissues.
    Can you believe that there are funeral halls that hand tissues to mourners?

    After coming outside, everyone writes letters.
    To the place of eternal darkness.
    To the place of eternal cold.
    To the place of eternal disappearance.

They write to promise to meet again, in another country, please.
They write to wish for peaceful rest, in another country, please.

Can killing God be this easy?
Lady No thinks on this Easter.
The people of this city wear funeral clothes.
The people of this city never smile.
The spring flowers of this city are particularly vulgar.
Lady No doesn't like these fully blossomed flowers.
Lady No doesn't like this pink that has ripened everywhere.

This city is now the funeral hall of Aerok.
Lady No goes to work at the funeral hall of Aerok.
Lady No teaches classes for sad students at the funeral hall.
Lady No writes documents she will send to the administration at the funeral hall.
Lady No looks at the sky that is grey like an ocean flipped over.

VACATION

Even in her sleep, Lady No is a teacher. She hates it because she is a teacher.

Voices, voices, voices that have left already are sitting on the chairs of her classroom.

It has been long since she opened her attendance book and pulled out ears from names.

The children took their bags and left, letting the wind carry their hair. None of it matters now.

The chairs broke, and pink butts have flown away.

To attendance books, grade books, exam books, and all these crumpled flying notebooks,

Lady No reads poems. Cold wind blows in the classroom.

What is the talking wind pushing into these ears?

On the blackboard, a broom from the closet and lunchboxes are rolling about.

And Lady No reads poems of Aerok for the blackboard in this dream!

Pages from books colder than the cold wind fly about in this classroom.

Fingers that ran across notebooks are gone, and words have fallen.

In the songs of today's children of Aerok, 'crazy' is a necessary word.

Why is Lady No a teacher even in a dream? She hates it because she is a teacher.

Glimmers of eyes densely packed on the chairs, falling outside the window.

The chairs and the desks are the frames of absence.

Where are the ears that drummed on the desk while listening to poems of Aerok?

Lady No is now a longing that no longer longs for things.

Lockers without keys weep with their mouths closed.

Lady No takes out the attendance book and calls on vibrating names.

Why am I a teacher even in my dream? I hate it because I am a teacher.

ONCE IT BECOMES WORDS, IT DISAPPEARS

Fictions often become films.

After watching a film based on a fiction, most people who have already read the fiction despair.

When you are reading fiction, the fiction's sentences switch on the space of imagined experience, but film makes that space small and limited.

Film can't handle how words can carry their lives into fiction and unfold the inside and the outside of their old time and space.

Therefore, Lady No likes fictions that can't be made into films.

Have you ever experienced a part of life getting turned into a part of a film or a narrative?

Have you ever paced aimlessly in a life that has become a part of a narrative?

Have you ever discerned what was expressed, and what was left unexpressed?

Have you ever experienced the sticky rain pouring into the warehouse of memories?

Confess! Confess! Confess!

Counseling will cure you. Counseling will console you. Counseling will make you better.

Counseling buses, draped in counseling banners, came to this city and pitched counseling tents. People swarmed them with manuals and pens in hand. Whenever buses drove by with banners on their sides reading, 'We Counsel,' Lady No thought about how frightened mothers and fathers must be, how hard it must be to speak up first; they must have buried themselves under quilts and wept.

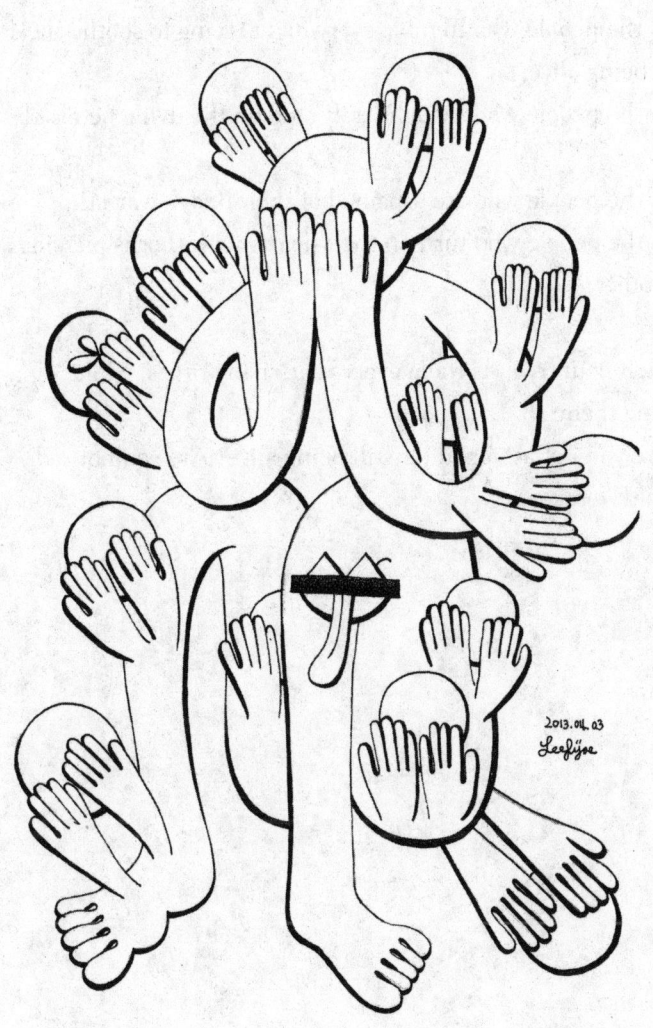

I LIVE IN AEROK

To the people for whom the scariest person is themselves,
To the people who tremble every night trying to soothe the sin of still being alive,
To the people who thoughtlessly step on the dying petals of flowers,
To the people who are ashamed of their body's warmth,
To the people who turn on their hearts with thorns piercing their bodies,

Their country asks them every year, many times, while whipping them,
"Are you not ashamed for still being alive? Are you not sad?"
To live in Aerok.

JUNE

TEARS OF EVEREST

Long ago, I visited Nepal.

It was before the incredible bloodshed between family members in the palace took place.

When rebels were everywhere asking which side you were on.

When every traveler had to keep cash in their pockets to bribe the rebels.

If you gave them cash even before they asked which side you were on, they gave you receipts.

They promised to pay you back when they took control.

One day, like any other day, the rebels blockaded the road we were on.

This time they did not ask for money.

They didn't even let us pass.

With no other option, after taking the long way around, travelers pooled some money together and got seats on a little propeller airplane.

We were running behind the departure time of our return plane to Aerok.

Our little propeller plane traced the famous peaks of Mount Everest between Nepal and Tibet.

It would be nicer to say that I wept for the sublime Everest that followed our small plane, but my tears were really for those incredibly sharp rocks that appeared in between the snow-covered peaks.

They seemed to be in so much pain, hanging up there in such high air. They were pain itself.

I wept so much I couldn't think about why I was weeping.

Since then, whenever I see snow-covered Everest on a screen, I weep.

Even before I can think about why I am weeping, those fierce rocks pierce the pit of my stomach.

TIME ERASER

The clock on her desk is Lady No's eraser.
It is very good at erasing the time of her room with each tick and tock.

She was sentenced to 7 years and was about to disappear behind the door.
"Hey _____!" Lady No called her by her name.
She turned around and looked at Lady No.
And then she shouted at Lady No, "You wanna die? Who do you think you are calling my name, you little—!"
The people in the courtroom on both sides laughed their butts off.

And decades later, when she got out and returned to the world, the air that surrounded her gradually changed from green to grey. Her green spirit and her sense of humor disappeared, and chaos held sway within her mind. She started sending terrifying emails and letters. This time, she got dressed in a hospital gown and disappeared behind iron doors. Lady No didn't call her name this time.

The beating of the time eraser is scarier than an actual beating.

The beating of the eraser is greater outside of a prison than inside.

The second hand on the desk ticks and tocks and passes, gripping its whip.

EXHIBITIONS OF A FEMALE ARTIST AND A MALE ARTIST

I visited two exhibitions at an art gallery located on Sukkgogae Street in Seocho District.

Here is an account of the paintings on the 2nd floor:

The face of a beheaded man wearing a crown, his upper torso naked. In front of him, a woman warrior, fashioned with a belt made of nine leather straps.

A woman installs a swing on Louise Bourgeois's Iron Spider and then rides the swing, only wearing red panties.

On the second floor of a foundry, a woman lies undressed.

Inside a deep tunnel hangs an iron mirror, and a woman is letting it reflect her naked body.

A cloud. But when you go near it, a body of a naked woman with a shaved head comes into view. They are tangled up with each other.

A white seal. But with a human face.

A white seal. It only has one face, but two bodies are attached to it. A Siamese seal.

The heels of her feet have evolved into ceramic high heels, a woman walking in the air.

Inside a white ceramic high heel, a woman's clitoris is opening its mouth.

After beheading her boyfriend, a woman sits like a pietà, and her room is red.

Thirty-six breasts are sewn on two large trumpets. From each breast grows an onion. The smell of onions rotting.

A woman is cutting up a fish. The kitchen is overflowing with heads and bodies of fishes.

Wearing owl masks, two girls are making love. Their bodies skinny.

Her whole body covered in mud, a woman cries. Her tears wash her.

Photographs of a real story. A healthy woman has surgery to become a man. There is a picture of them from before and after the surgery. In the same room, in front of the same mirror, in the same position. Black hair grows on their pink chest. Next to this photo, there is another photo where black hair is covering their breasts completely. They are transitioning from being woman to man.

It appears they are drawing their self-consciousness, which refused to be hurt inside their body. It looks like an ear sewn up with black threads.

A girl in the water gave birth to a red baby. The girl is holding her baby. Upon a closer look, the girl turns out to be a ghost.

In a library, a big woman is completely undressed and lying on books piled up a meter high. Skinny women who have come to borrow books are observing the big woman.

Hanging up a photograph on a wall, trying to be like what's in the photograph, becoming that body through starvation. But the longer the starvation goes on, a tail grows from the body. The tail thickens.

Lady No was the only visitor of the 2nd-floor gallery. There were no flower garlands.

Next, the exhibition on the 1st floor:

Six teacups and a saucer.
White porcelain jar.
A slightly bigger white porcelain jar.
An even bigger white porcelain jar.
A very big white porcelain jar.
A white porcelain with an inscription that reads "Peaceful Reunification."
A white porcelain with a drawing of a bird.
A white porcelain with a drawing of a fish.

A white porcelain with a drawing of a tiger.

A moon jar.

Another six teacups and a saucer.

A bowl with a lotus flower pattern.

A bowl with a comb pattern.

A bowl.

A bowl.

A bowl.

A jar.

A jar.

A jar.

A teacup.

A teacup.

A teacup.

<People And Places Who Sent Flower Garlands>

Minister of Unification, Mr. Ryu X Yik

Special Vice-minister, Mr. Kwon X Gi

President of The Society of Aerok Lawyers, Mr. Shin X Mu

Governor of North Kyungsang Province, Mr. Kim X Yong

Pastor of Myungsung Church, Kim X Hwan

Samji Accounting Firm

Seoul National University Law School, Professor Jeong X Sub

Chairman of Aerok Broadcasting System, Yi X Young

The Legal Research and Training Institute, Researcher Kim X Wook

Nonghyup Bank, CEO, Mr. Shin X Shik

ET CETERA

Visitors: 12 Neckties, and 2 Old Ladies Who Have Grown Old

THE SOUL OF AN OBJECT

The car let Lady No sit inside it for a decade, and now it is gone.

No one else but Lady No had ever held the car's wheel, until the car drove past Lady No.

The soul of the car peered out at Lady No as it left her.

Lady No's eyes captured this scene like a camera.

And now the scene keeps repeating.

Like a grandfather who had to let go of his dear old cow from his stable, Lady No would like to drag smoke deeply from a long tobacco pipe.

The morning after, thousands of miles away,

Lady No's car was seen as it began to ride off toward somewhere far.

As far away as someone sailing to a distant country.

Piercing the air of ultramarine daybreak.

A video message from the soul of an object.

DEVOTION INDEX

There is a graph with the names of faculty members.
An index shows how many of your students got employed at companies that offer full benefits.
Of course, there is not a single round sticker above Lady No's name.
There was at least a single star sticker on one of Lady No's poetry books.
Lady No searches online for how to write a letter of resignation.

The higher-ups at the administration demand that since you couldn't get anyone employed, at least prove your devotion.
Come to work every day, even during vacation, and encourage your students' job hunting.
Call up businesses, set up meetings.
And prove that these meetings took place by taking photographs and submitting them every week.
For whom do we perform this devotion? For the higher-ups? For her students writing away in their little rooms?

Someone from the Department of Music, after failing to get anyone employed, calls up one of their students.
"You must get employed where they provide health insurance," they insisted.
The student answered,
"I want to play drums for the rest of my life.
Isn't that what you taught me to do, teacher?"
Even if they couldn't get them employed, they must have a meeting every week and take photos.
Devotion must be evaluated.

After making stir-fried potatoes, Lady No wonders, 'How will the higher-ups of my family evaluate my devotion?"

After writing a poem, she wonders, 'How will His Royal Highness the Reader the Noble and the Wise evaluate my poem's devotion?'

After meeting her friend, Lady No asks them, 'My right honorable friend, what score will you give me for my devotion that I have spent on the advancement of our friendship?'

Lady No begins to develop obsessive compulsion about having her devotion evaluated every moment.

Lady No must show devotion to the administration every year.

She must show her devotion instead of her letter of resignation.

She must show devotion to the administration's order to get her students employed after having raised them as artists.

TIME RETURNS AS AN ITCH

One of my arms began to itch.
I unfolded a wire hanger and slipped it into my arm's plaster cast.
Once I started to scratch that itch, I couldn't stop.

I scratched until I was bleeding.
Even when I got on a bus, I thought about scratching the arm as soon as I got home.

People stared at my plastered arm.
Which made me want to scratch it even more. I didn't know until then that getting stared at could be such an itch.

When I wasn't scratching, I was holding my shoulder.
I thought that if I held my arm, it would itch even more.

Every moment was like hearing news about an ex-lover,
How my body pricks up! My itchy arm tenses up as if it has ears.

There are two kinds in this world: the itchy and the not-itchy.
For example, buses are itchy, and streetlamps are itchy,
Even puddles are itchy, and the sun is itchy,
But the wind is that rare thing, the not-itchy, and the raindrops are extremely itchy, and that is how they are categorized.

If I tried to endure the itch, my whole body is flooded with pain.
The space between the skin of my head and the skull hurt the most.
The world was hiding the itch beneath the surface of pain.

I lifted heavy things to forget the itch.
I ran all day to forget the itch.

But when my patience was exhausted, I looked for something pointy. If I wanted to liberate the itch, I had to start scratching.

I scratched so much, I feared I would scratch myself down to my bones, so I went to a hospital.
Please take off this cast.
I can't stand it anymore.
The doctor told me.
Please don't come here anymore.
Don't you know you don't have an arm?

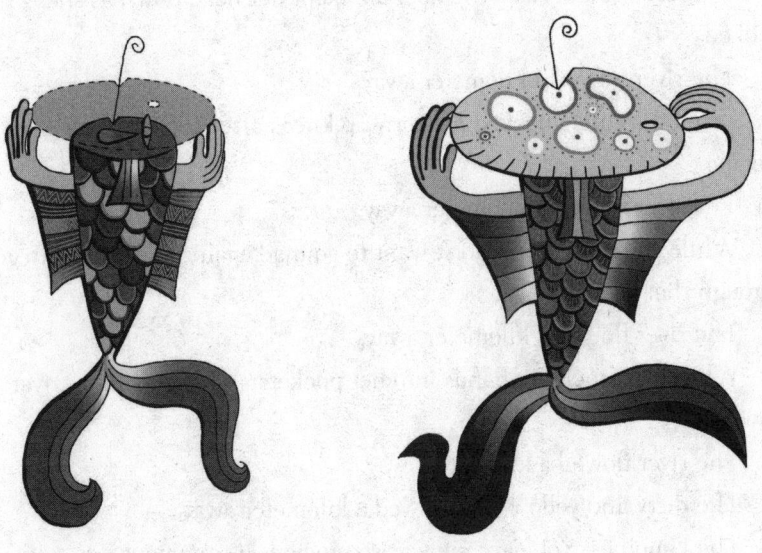

BY THE RIVER OUSE

While Virginia was tying up the strings of her fur coat
The river flowed a kilometer away.
While Virginia closed the door and kept her head down as she walked
The river flowed a kilometer away.
While Virginia checked her torn-up knees after tripping over a stone
The river flowed a kilometer away.
While she mumbled I don't want to go mad again I don't want to go through that again
The river flowed a kilometer away.
While she stuck her hands into her pockets and watched the river flow
The river flowed a kilometer away.
The dirty and yellow river flowed a kilometer away.
The happiness you gave me was so precious, so precious—
The words in her final will were read, and in all that time
The river flowed a kilometer away.
Into your crumbling shape I pushed myself in feet first.
How unfortunate you were while trying to hold my life together.
I flowed a kilometer into you.
Even after everyone else had left, you protected me till the end,
And now I am letting you go and flowing a kilometer into you.

The pill bottles hitting one another inside the river
The pills bejewel the lips, shining and flowing in fullness.

The past is already no longer.
The future isn't yet.
Therefore, the present isn't now.

Virginia's river was like a quilt for the days, and it flowed and carried Virginia's cane.

The river stopped like a mirror before continuing its flow, piercing Lady No's eyes.

The river that will drown all the rooms of women scattered all over the world.

THIN COUNTRY

Barely there air.
Barely there freedom.
Barely there existence.

When I go to Tibet, I feel as though I am in a country where poetry lives.

Tall and stout men and high-spirited women keep their bodies close to the earth as they move toward the temple.
Their thick, black-braided hairs are long.

The smell of burning yak butter and the sound of monks chanting the sutras.
Their thick horn-rimmed glasses and their clamorous talking styles.
The words of Buddha recited while spinning prayer wheels during their walks.
When Baek Seok passed through colonized Aerok's market streets, he smelled his country becoming barely there, and you can smell it here, too.

Just outside the busy parts of the city, there are people's black tents. The hard labor of paving roads has rubbed away their bodies.
Inside the tents are bowls with teas someone forgot to finish. Plastic bags roll about. Their glossy black eyes.

Black dirt underneath their fingernails, they grasp powdered barley from bowls.
And after breaking brick-hard tea leaves, throw them together into a kettle.

Barely there air here makes Lady No fall into a meditative state multiple times a day.

When Lady No lies down or sits, she levitates.

She levitates when she walks up the staircases of a building, too.

In the barely there air, going up the floors is as tough as climbing up a mountain.

Her body has never felt heavier before. Lady No thinks that she might as well be dragging Earth behind her when she walks.

And for the briefest of moments, Lady No breaks away from Lady No and watches Lady No deep in meditation.

In the middle of the night, Lady No opens the window of her old inn.

She loses her sense of time as she watches an open window of someone's house from which anonymous light is pouring out.

Beneath the black sky, black hairs have gone to sleep, and a barely there ghost's oily hair flies between them.

Sitting on red chairs stuck to the temple's walls,
Their legs resting on red carpets,
Men of this country are deep in their discussions. She looks at them from above.
Black kettle boiling with the tea they are drinking all night, cigarette smoke drifting.

As if one has come to a country where poetry lives,
Barely there air.
Barely there civilization.
Barely there Lady No.

FAR BEYOND

In the vertigo treatment clinic's waiting room, there was a grandmother who would talk to anyone, and because of her, conversations blossomed.

The words we used most were

Cliff,
Bluff,
Crag,
Slope,
And ground below.

It was a list.

In the physical therapy room, we practiced how to live and not fall off precipices.

Walking on one leg, turning one's head while staying focused on a single point, standing without falling on a shaking plank, clapping to the signal while on a moving plank, lying on a bed cut up into squirming pieces, spinning one's butt while riding an exercise ball, vibrating one's whole body on a vibrating waterbed.

All these activities are far beyond doable for people standing on cliffs.

The infinity is right beneath our feet. We usually place our bodies inside fog and winds and trees and sunshine and others of the empty air, but we place our feet on the ground. But our feet, alas, are in disharmony with the ground.

The precariousness of this tiny real estate we've been granted on this earth, feeling as if we are on someone's palm, as if that is the exact amount, even that little bit that will be stolen soon from us.

As if all our present moments are leaping off the cliff every second. As if loss is ongoing.

MAMMAL

Before the Jokhang Temple in Lhasa, where the air is thin,
I am having an out-of-body experience. And so,
As I watch myself prostrating,
All I can think of is how heavy this mammal's body must be.
No matter. This sadness is a transparent disinterest. A kind of gaze.

Lama monks, dressed in white aprons,
Swing blades shaped like half-moons and rectangles
And tenderize the body of the dead.
But the eagles show no signs of favor.
They are annoyed that this
Is what they are getting after being invited here.
Lady No, who comes from a lower town,
Must taste horrible,
And for the first time in her life, she wants to look good for eagles.

Why is Lady No a mammal that shits and sucks on tits?
Why is Lady No an animal with hot fingers and sticky sweat?
Why is Lady No a female whose tits spill out at loud noises?
Such a burden to carry in life.
The smell of Lady No is so stinky that she fears smelling flowers, afraid her breath might kill them.

(Why does Lady No have these two long arms?
Please do not give me flowers.
We all come from the earth,

But here is this single blossom of a flower,
Barely opening her eyes after rising from the earth.
If Lady No touches her,
A moment might turn into brutality.
I can't even dare to stand next to a wide-open flower.)

IMPORTED ALIBI

Lady No is reading his book.
He summarizes foreign critical theories and shares them with her.
He seems to be a merchant of theories.
This must be his profession.
As the publishing houses of Aerok translate and publish certain books,
the copyright prices of certain foreign writers start to increase.
However, Aerok's books are rarely translated into other languages.
Sometimes, the translations are subpar.
This isn't because the translators lack skills in the other country's language.
Rather, it's because they are not proficient in Aerok's language, according to Professor H.
Every few years in Aerok, it becomes fashionable to idolize certain foreigners.
When she was writing her academic thesis, Lady No faced criticism from her teachers for not citing these idols enough. Some theses were rejected for the lack of idol citations.
Even poets are expected to cite figures from abroad in their work.
While talking to a highly respected writer from France,
Lady No inquired about a writer who is often cited in Aerok.
The French writer grumpily answered, "Isn't that writer just a lump of gravy?" This shocked her.
In Aerok these days, critics and academics can hardly claim to be intellectuals if they do not cite that writer,
whose work often acts as an alibi for Aerok's literature.
We are constantly looking for an alibi to speak nothing about the present, preferring instead to look abroad or to the past.

Yet, the French writer's laughter was similar to how the people of Aerok mock Aerok's intellectuals.

Until that moment, Lady No had thought the disparaged "lump-of-gravy" writer, scorned by the French writer, would perfectly serve as an alibi for her writing—even if it was an alibi imported from abroad.

THE SUN KING'S CHAIRS

There was a poetry reading at the largest castle in France, built 500 years ago.
The great hall of the castle was adorned with full-body portraits of the Sun King and medieval paintings.

It was the day after my arrival in France.
I was exhausted from jet lag.
Long chairs lined the walls of the hall,
covered in deep crimson carpets with vivid threads so striking, I pondered their color as I placed my bag upon one and rested.

After resting, we recited poems in Aerok's language and French.

Once the reading concluded, the castle's custodian approached me discreetly.
"The long chair you were lying on is 500 years old.
It's one of the Sun King's chairs," he whispered.
"I didn't intervene earlier because I understood you're from afar, but those chairs are meant for viewing, not sitting."

Shocked, Lady No apologized profusely, bowing repeatedly.
But to leave those chairs carelessly out like that.
Everyone in her group had sat on them.

Afterward, merely the mention of the castle's name made her grovel and bow.
She completely forgot about the poetry reading and the like.

CIRCLE

If you stay at home cooking all day,
just the sight of anything round makes you nauseous.
Round bowls, round pots, round pans, round water, round time, round reincarnation.
Lady No quickly tries to picture a square desk, a square book, a square blackboard, a square classroom.
When you're inside a square, you think of a circle; when you're inside a circle, you think of a square.
If God can't make a square,
Lady No once thought, then He must not be inside the square.
Lady No cries out in front of the square sink,

I really hate circles!

Circles are the mold made to keep us serving this world, day after day, never escaping!

A circle is zero, a hand pushing us into zero. Zero multiplied by nothing. It's foam. It's a balloon. It's a boundary. It's the present moment, endlessly dissolving.

Whether it's a square or a circle, you can't escape.
It comes back endlessly. It's already passed, yet it returns. The morning from a hundred years ago returns. The evening from a thousand years ago returns.
Shapes are the molds that trap us. It's reincarnation.

Carried by the slingshot of the sun, we race through and past. We return.

After raising her head to look at the night sky, two starlights, long since dead, finally reach Lady No's eyes. The vanished past shines at last. Where could we possibly escape to?

YET UNBORN

Lady No left Lady No and levitated. Then she looked down, and what she saw was merely Lady No's body.

She had been in pain, but once she looked at herself after levitating out of her, she didn't seem so pitiful.

She seemed to be in shock, but not too much of a shock.

She was an objet, a thing that some artist didn't finish making, crushing it instead.

But the thing was far more worn out than she had expected.

A pale body that looked like Lady No was enduring. Lady No was slowly becoming a balloon losing its air.

The moment she wondered if she might be a butterfly flying out of her chrysalis, Lady No was back in her body. She was all shocks and thumps as she landed into her body.

Afterwards, she thought that whatever it was that had levitated in such a way could not be called a soul. A soul could not be so quotidian. There was nothing noble in how it looked down at its own body. Gazing like a stranger, Lady No had looked at Lady No like a person turned into a mirror. Lady No who left Lady No was a stranger filled with pity and shame. Lady No who levitated into the air was the secular gaze of a stranger.

In her notebook, Lady No wrote down that what happened was her experience of turning into a mirror. In a reality that was not reality, at a place that was not a place, Lady No who wasn't Lady No had watched Lady No during this experience. It was the upside-down, master-and-visitor switching experience between Lady No and a place called mirror. It was like how the speaker in the poem observes the quotidian 'I', and it was like an echo looking back into the throat, and that is how Lady No stayed awhile in that virtual space.

Afterwards, whenever she watched a butterfly, she came to think that the butterfly must be very distant from the memory and the identity of having been a larva under earth. And that since Lady No still had her legs on the ground, she was still a larva. And that her roots haven't been uprooted.

Come to think of it, it seems Lady No is yet unborn.

THE VOICE OF A WART

He loved the voice he heard from inside his body.

Perhaps, when he was alone, he may have feared the voice, but when he was with Lady No he liked to show it off and say things like,

You call yourself a poet and you can't even hear the voice? What are you even writing?

Lady No answered,

Does your Lord Voice sing you a poem, too?

No, the voice tells me how all the scholars of this world will kneel before me.

Lady No dragged him to a hospital.

He told the doctor in a booming voice like an orator about the voice he was hearing.

The voice comes from my wart.

Auditory hallucinations are like colds, the doctor said, it will go away quickly once you take medicine.

After hearing the diagnosis, he ran out of the room faster than a rabbit.

What was his fear when he was so proud?

He had no desire to escape the voice.

It seemed he was more fearful of the world washed clean of the voice.

Lady No ran after him but couldn't figure out where he was hiding.

Later she took him to a traditional medicine clinic instead of the hospital he feared so much.

In every black birthmark of my body, a voice lives, he said.

He threw away the medicine from the traditional clinic into a trash can.

(She found out later.)

The voice grew louder. He became half of a being, his mind lost to the voice.

Later, the voice shouted profanities relentlessly.

And so, he spoke to Lady No while mixing profanities with the voice from inside his body.

The following line is a summary of what he said.

Please just take out the voice that is tormenting me. But leave the voice that I like.

But the voice cannot be taken out in parts, it can only get stronger as a whole,

Its parts do not act independently, the doctor said.

He went beyond the unknown world, toward a more ruinous place.

Lady No begged him to remove his birthmarks and his wart, but it was useless.

Hanging onto his wart, he rose to heights higher than Lady No could comprehend.

Whenever she was with him, Lady No reached the wet and soft well in her dream and faced the echoes clawing up from the well's bottom and emerging. Her body trembled. For he had made Lady No hear the voice of that place.

LIVING IN LEAVING

You've left, but your afterimage remains.

A poet is someone who lives in a country of afterimages.

When you place your hand into a blurry face, the face will slice you like a knife.

Perhaps it is a country of 0.0001 second.

That country.

The country of leaving.

The poet lives in that country.

Even though it seems to not exist in this world, it is there for real, shining on our memories, shining on our imaginations, shining on our dreams, this blurry sun, rising over the country, over the country of silence, and the poet is a citizen of that country.

The moment you leave, the moment when your shadow turns the corner, that moment, that is when poetry is living in leaving. Your hair, your nape, and the way they are when you turn the corner. Their tedious repetition. The poet lying on their side draws their face and knees closer together. The poet's body becomes rounder. In that moment, is the poet in the condition of 'being dead' or is it you who are in the condition of 'being dead'? Can death be a condition expressed in present-progressive form? It would be wrong to do so in a country of grammatical rules, but it is possible in the country of afterimages, of death's progression. The eternal progression. You and the poet are now 'being dead.' The 'I' in the poem hugs their body making it round as it is 'being dead.' The moment you turned the corner, 'I' died. It is like when the boy on a bicycle, after getting hit by a truck, was lying on a hospital bed. The boy rewatched that brief yet lengthy moment again and again. The truck driver slammed the brake, and a small white car appeared in the boy's view, and after breaking through that car's windshield, the boy levitated. The boy watched that scene, and only that scene, again and again. He watched it fourteen thousand and four hundred and forty-four times on a single day. The moment when he and an object crashed. Within that moment in time, the boy is dead and thus alive. And so, here is a country in which a moment flows eternally, a country of poetry, a blurry country, a country blurry as if it is a light shining on a memory. The poet is the citizen of that blurry country. The present continuing eternally. The nothing time. The person who still lives in the afterimage of an event after the location of the event has been thoroughly cleaned up. The person who feels the beating, rowdy heart of an afterimage. The moment of leaving the 'I', the citizen of that moment is 'I', the citizen of an afterimage. S/he is a poet.

QUESTIONS

I went to an international book fair.
Journalists from Aerok came, too.
One of them asked Lady No a question.
What is your impression of attending this book fair?
Lady No answered.
Yes, my impression (journalists love that word!). I feel like a poet who has come to a market to sell poems.
Can you tell us the list of your published books of poetry?
Please look it up on web portals.
The same journalist asked again.
What is your major work?
Not sure. Why don't you look it up online?
Another journalist asked.
Which works of yours have been translated?
Please look it up on foreign web portals.
What is the response to your work in foreign countries?
Please look it up on foreign web portals.
What is your next work?
I haven't finished writing it yet so I can't tell you.
An angered journalist left.

Next, a foreign moderator asked.
Is there censorship in Aerok?
(That again, ugh, that's so in the past.)
Now that military dictatorship has disappeared in Aerok, how do you write poetry without oppression?
Then how do the poets of your country write poetry when they have never experienced military dictatorships?

(Were they trying to show off how great their country is, were they even showing contempt of Aerok?)

Last question. If you couldn't write anymore, then what would you do?

A fiction writer sitting next to Lady No answered. Visibly confused.

You can still read though, can't you? I will keep reading.

Respect soared in Lady No's heart for that writer with whom she had left Aerok.

THE HOST OF DEATH

A rat infected with a cat parasite called toxoplasma gondii
Will only choose actions that will get them eaten by a cat.
Even though it looks like a rat,
Its brain gets re-wired to activate the long-term project of becoming cat food.
Waiting before Lord Cat's house when Lord Cat is hungry,
Going into heat only when smelling Lord Cat's piss
Waiting at Lord Cat's trash cans before Lord Cat gets there.

Jaroslav Flegr is a cat parasite researcher.
He was infected with the cat parasite toxoplasma gondii.
He started to live like an infected rat without realizing it.
He walked slowly,
His footsteps led him into areas infested with cats.

A human infected with the cat parasite toxoplasma gondii
Supposedly develops schizophrenia with a mind of a rat.
Lady No, a human who likes to talk in the mode of a rat speaker in this poem, might be such a case.

Perhaps all living things are infected with parasites of death, the spores of air.
We drink air relentlessly.
But it is the air that eventually kills us.
We breathe air 15 times every 60 minutes every 24 hours,
Eventually getting infected with the spores of air and growing old and dying.
(We drink around 108,000 liters of air every day

Meaning we gulp down about a deep well's worth of air every day.)
And so, people who have drunk air in droves have faces
Befitting of death.

All poets wear faces infected with death's toxoplasma gondii.
Death is ready to devour them for what only they will choose to do.
On the outside, they seem fine but their brains
Are infected with radical unreality, absence of existence, and constant new birth of extinction.
The poets activate every day their long-term projects to become death.
Pickled in farewells going extinct every moment, they whine all day.
Despite their constant defeat against the undefeated extinction
They are infected by its seduction and drift towards death's door.
And so, thrashing every day, wanting to die before death, the poets are the infected.

MOTHERS

Like a cow pulling out her body's reserves and eating it again,
the evening sun treads upon her own body's path of red earth with
heavy steps.
Over a mountain ridge, throwing
a bucket of shit out of sheer boredom.

A big noise is enough
for a mother's engorged breasts to overflow, and
she is my mother, younger than myself, who
teaches elementary school children,
checks for head lice, and writes the school bulletin for parents.
She carries an empty, clanging lunchbox
on her journey back here, to home.

A cow burdened beyond her capacity
cannot even find death!
Bulging to the point of bursting,
nipples are dragged across the gravel road.
The solitary sun's droplets of blood fall,
soaking into the earth beneath the hooves.

After the sun descends into what lies beyond,
mothers who give birth to darkness quietly return, step by step.

WITCH-TYPE POET

They name her Female Poet Lady No or Woman Poet Lady No instead of calling her Lady No. These names aren't mere suggestions that she is a poet who happens to be a woman. Based on a narrow definition of standardized womanhood, petrified by conventional social sensibilities, those who name her as such imply something about her on a deeper level, that she enjoys using language in a 'womanly' way. However, even if all the sentences of this world could be gendered, a woman poet's poem doesn't possess a unique way of commanding womanly sentences. We can't simply judge a poet's work to be womanly poetry written from a woman's perspective only because the poet is a woman. Once you name a poet a woman poet, then manly poetry becomes the standard, and womanly poetry becomes its provincial other. This does not happen as often to fiction writers. It is rare they are named a woman writer or a female writer.

Naming has had a long life. Naming is an instrument with which identity is branded. Some critics keep on dividing identities. Witch-type Woman Poet, Shaman-type Woman Poet, Whore-type Woman Poet, Girl-type Woman Poet, Mother-type Woman Poet. Man Poets are not categorized as such. They are not named Gigolo-type Man Poet, Magician-type Man Poet, Shaman-type Man Poet, Boy-type Man Poet, Soldier-type Man Poet, or Father-type Man Poet. Man Poets are not named with adjectives, careers, and styles. They are just poets. Lady No is called Witch-type Poet. Witches reject normalcy, get abortions, and encourage adultery. They can disappear at burning stakes, ride on black horses, kidnap someone and bring them along for the ride. (In a Charles Bukowski story, a witch reduces a man down to 15 centimeters. This story could be a terrifying fable about a wife who considers her man a mere sex toy, or it could be a caricature of wives who have no love left.) But didn't all the witches get burned at the stake? How are they still being born, still growing up, still living? This is because categorizing comes from the intent to rule, control, and judge. And have you considered what happens to the poets whose gender identities exclude them from all such categories?

Instead of categorizing poets, Lady No thinks it is better to categorize poems. Using the poem's imagery, use of rhythm, the speaker's tone, the invention of form, et cetera, et cetera. But perhaps because of the current climate, Lady No can't help but think more about women. She even thinks, 'How can a poet who hasn't transited through womanliness ever be called a poet?' It is really difficult to talk about women using women's language. Because there is no women's language. Because we must first take the language that Man Poets use, then fillet it like a raw fish before we can use it. Is it easy to turn cooked back into raw? Is it easy to be a cat with Asperger's devouring the remorseless dictionary of her mother tongue? Therefore, a woman poet must always begin again. She must offer up her poem as a sacrifice to the expansion of poetry.

For example, saying 'They lived well, and their family was happy' is an expression that has devoured womanly language. It has swallowed up women's emotions and situations. Women's language can't adhere to the writing manuals that confuse objectivity and group mentality. Because women do not possess their own language, they have no choice but to let the language of men gallop through their bodies. Thus, the content and form of women's poetry seem ill-fitting. With such misfitting frames and grains, a Woman Poet will be accused of spewing nonsense that sounds like a ghost peeling and eating rice seeds. Woman Poets, how pathetic.

Because the history of women's poetry is so short, the space of women's poetry is the new world. Woman Poets have always lived there. But sly Man Poets steal even this new world, too. Woman Poets must discover and depart for another new world and unfurl and wave their primitive flag. They must, because even their wombs and breasts have been taken from them. Still, it is true that compared to the Man Poets who swing their masculinity around and liken women to food, the Man Poets who are equipped with false wombs are a lot cuter. Lady No would like to get out of the category of the Woman Poet and fly like a seagull and shriek. Because when she sits still in her room too long with her thoughts, an unconscionable amount of womanliness springs forth from this poet sister.

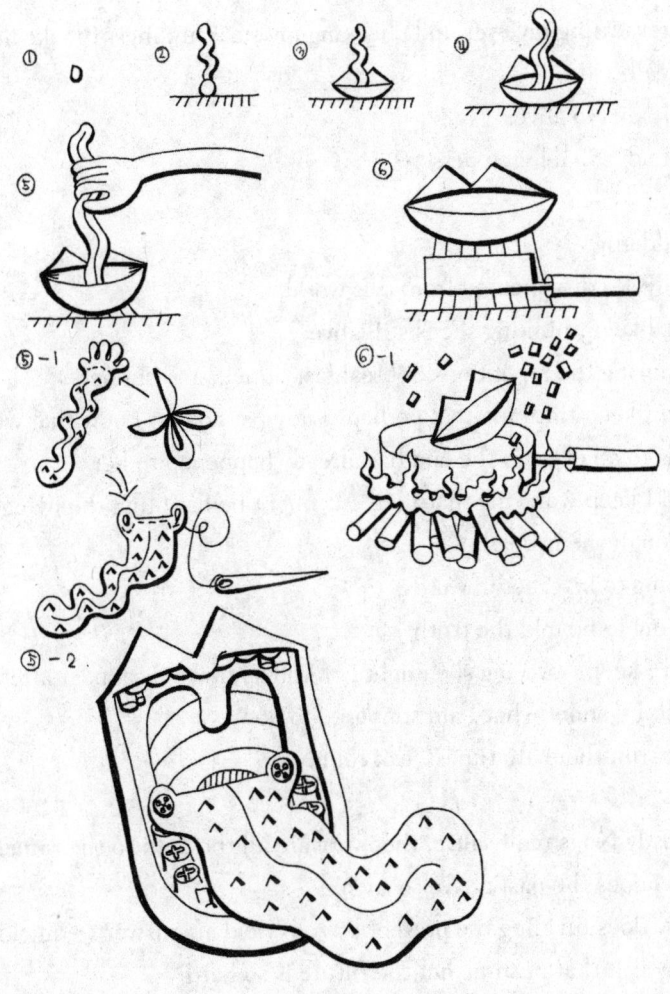

ASYMPTOTIC CURVE

After raising my eyes and checking my surroundings, I make a phone call.
Is Lady No alive?
Is Lady No a living person?

Suddenly
Lady No disappeared from this world
but I keep thinking she is still alive
enduring the repetitions of breakfast, lunch, and supper,
and I keep thinking that perhaps Lady No doesn't know that what happens to all of us in the end has already happened to her,
and I keep worrying that Lady No might be haunting the living even though she is dead,
asking to be exact in words,
asking to be told the truth,
and I keep worrying she might not know how to disappear after dying, so I wonder what I am supposed to do.
But still, there are times I ask calmly.

If Lady No is really alive, then why are all the days so the same?
Why does the past arrive so soon?
Why does dividing the present by zero yield an answer so quickly?
Why is it that pushing out the future is so hard?
Why can't one be curious about the last pages of the fiction one is living in?
There are times I really want to ask these questions to someone.

Could Earth be a shadow or a hell of a certain star?
Could it be a transmigrating soul wondering in the shadow world?

If that is the case, then I want to bite into the roses blooming over someone else's wall
And vomit a red broth, like water where soap has dissolved.

Ah, but now, perhaps because I just came out of a 36.5 degrees Celsius body, I am trembling.

LECTURE AND PROTEST

Lady No lectures a poet from Africa about how to brew and drink tea.
First, she explains the color and the shape of the cup.
Then, she suggests that he should feel the cup in his hands.
And then, she talks about the temperature of the water used for brewing.
She says that he should wait for the boiling water to cool.
He listens without making a move.
And then takes turns staring at the hands and lips of Lady No.
Lady No tells him to take pleasure in the scent and the hue of the tea.
After finishing her lecture, Lady No pours him a cup.
With his very big hand, he holds up a teacup that is smaller than his eyes, drinks from it, and then says to Lady No,
Myself, my family, and my friends, we cannot afford to have a moment like this.
We have no leisure like this.
This light, this scent, you can only do this when there is time to rest.
If my people had time like this, we wouldn't be in a war.
He asks Lady No if the people of Aerok have a lot of time.
And he tells her that you drink tea like this only when the war is over.
He meant that he would never drink it again.

JULY

VOWELS

I I I I I
Crying the pituitary and pineal glands and the brain.
E E E E E E
Crying the ear, nose and throat, and thyroid.
A A A A A A
Crying the lungs.
YO YO YO YO YO YO
Crying the middle of chest.
O O O O O O
Crying the liver and stomach
OE OE OE OE OE OE
Crying the diaphragm
WI WI WI WI WI WI
Crying the kidney
U U U U U U
Crying the anus and genitals.
OM OM OM OM OM OM
Crying the heart.

Vowels are connected to the balloons of the body.

Lady No has a bad habit. She likes to guess which of your bones and organs are crying when you speak with your mouth open.

Lady No listens to how the organs of your body come together to play like an orchestra.

Musical instruments cry from inside your head and body. Your vocal cords pull tougher all those sounds and itself cries. Who is seducing you so as to make you spit out such beautiful harmony?

Upon hearing those cries, the consonants in your oral cavity respond with their own crying.

Waves roll in, and the moon drifts away.

THAT WOMAN'S KITCHEN

No one visits her kitchen for a meal.
Even after a three-hour hike on a trail, returning just in case,
Even after a few laps in the swimming pool,
Even after sweating profusely in a sauna,
Her kitchen silently decays like stagnant bilge water.
Flames never kiss the pots, cups remain untouched by lips, and
No footprints mar the floor.
Spilled cups remain unreturned to their places in this kitchen.
The kitchen's guardian, who has long forgotten how to announce
"it's time to eat,"
watches over it.
Dust accumulates into small mounds in the filter, and
No one dries their hands on an apron after daily dishwashing, nor
Does anyone raise their voice to fill an empty cup,
Attempting to sing, only for bubbles to emerge instead,
In this kitchen as silent as a fishbowl.

Though no lumps like potatoes have ever gone on a plate,
Rotten vegetables are discarded and replaced daily, and
Even the kitchen's woman does not dine here.
Should the cupboard still be opened? Above, clouds drift and planes fly,
Seemingly offering the freedom to lift a verb, pairing it with an adverb,
Yet the fear of someone's arrival, now that the door stands open, lingers,
So without ever saying "Eat as much as you like!"
She gazes daily at her own reflection in the dish.

The woman folds napkins into fish, fruit, and people who dine.
Whenever she returns home, she poops little black poops like a rat.
She cleans the table, purchases flowers, but
Like ennui stretching miles through each street,
An onion in a glass sprouts roots alarmingly,
And seaweed under the sink dances, yet
She alone, smiling, imagines saying "I'll make it just for you,"
Dreaming of frying fish leaping in a pot, mimicking the sound of rain,
But, stumbling in fish shoes and holding a fish bag,
There is a woman who frees all the fish into the rainy streets.

EVEN IN FRONT OF WOULD-BE WRITERS

We must all be a brand.
The teacher said with his arms resting on the high podium.
Your brand marketing must begin right at this moment.
The teacher said.

If you become a brand your name will be on the walls of subway stations.
They will be glued to the banners on buses.

A nation is a brand.
A writer is a brand.
Even a dog is a brand.

Do you know who created the greatest brand for a nation?
Think about it.

Before you, the people of the earth await, and they are consumed with desire
To be haunted by the ghosts of brands.
Let us all become brands, whatever it takes.
The teacher on high wiped his sweat.

Do you know which brand is the greatest among
The brands that tell you not to get seduced by brands?
He shouted.

In front of would-be writers, he talked about sentimental-type brand, pure-and-sweet-type brand, sexy-type brand, wild-man-type brand, exotic-type brand, multifaceted-type brand, naïve-type brand, femme-fatale-type brand—he illustrated the paradox with examples.

WHEN WILL WE FINISH THIS PRACTICE?

Someone in the unit upstairs is playing the piano.

They are practicing a piece that people in this country typically play when they first begin learning piano. From morning to evening, the playing never ceases.

Unless the pianist believes that she will save the world with her piano playing, the incessantly passionate practice remains inexplicable.

Lady No thinks of a girl locked away in her room all day, focused and unwavering.
No school, no meals, no restroom breaks, only the piano. If she makes a mistake, she replays that section relentlessly until it's perfect. A certain maestro likely underwent the same process. No one can achieve mastery without navigating through this clumsy, obsessive rhythm. Until they overcome these rhythmic waves, no one can embrace the freedom of natural performance. As Lady No listens to the girl's piano playing, her heart flutters with concern that the girl will repeat her usual error. As her playing nears that part, Lady No's heart starts to vibrate, her fingertips tremble, her head and shoulders develop tics. But the girl upstairs falters again.

Unable to bear it anymore, Lady No's roommate pleads with the upstairs neighbor to cover the floor beneath the piano with soundproof padding.

After a few days, the piano's sound is muffled as if it's enveloped in a quilt.

This change leads Lady No to listen even more intently to the music. This new, subdued sound touches her nerves more than the previous loud notes. Her head and shoulder tics worsen.

Please adhere to the noise-level regulation hours as stated in our apartment building rulebook, she requests.

The piano can now only be heard from 9 AM to 9 PM.

Lady No imagines the girl again. Perhaps she's a girl made to feel ugly by the world. A girl bullied by her classmates. A beaten girl. A crying girl. A girl with disheveled hair. Her only friend, the practice song for the piano. A girl who never attends school.

Lady No weeps in her bed. Even late into the night, her memories can't be found in the bag of her past, replaced instead by the clumsy, simple melody of the piano song. Lady No's mind can't travel to the past or the future. The piano sound and the memory gaps it causes are all that remain. The bright halo that once encompassed the past seems shattered. Time's gentle flow appears disrupted. Lady No's times transform into those practice songs. Now, Lady No seems memory-less, left only with the slow strikes of those clumsy fingers hitting the empty air.

The practice of that famous song induces nausea when she hears the first few notes each morning. Headache. This auditory torture permeates the home's barriers. Lady No hears it even when she's outside. On nights when the sound ceases, hallucinatory sounds replace it. Not a single moment passes gently. When the sound concludes, anxiety intensifies. It's as if the sound has been implanted into her body. During her lecture,

Lady No starts to mimic the song's score on her desk. She begins to avoid her home, to hate it. The objects in her home seem foreign, those on her desk seem like they belong to a stranger. She spends more time outside. When she does return home, she listens to famous piano tracks in succession. But when that music ends, the practice song bubbles up in her mind, overwhelming any other piano music. Eric Satie's Gymnopédies is nothing more than delicate mist against the thunderous practice song that storms her brain. Lady No decides to watch TV all day, memorizing all the names of girl group idols. She aims to meticulously fill out their profile dictionary and create graphs depicting their event schedules. Like the girls of this generation, Lady No strives to fill her memory bank with idols' music and dance, rather than her own memories.

But one midday, unable to tolerate it anymore, she rings the upstairs neighbor's doorbell. The practice song, audible even from the doorstep, abruptly halts when the bell rings. Then, the sound of a chair being pushed. Slippers dragging on the floor. A face appears when the door opens—an elderly woman on the brink of a nervous breakdown.

Lady No reflects as she lies in her bed that night. She considers the light slumbers of two women, one upstairs and one downstairs, both nearing their respective breakdowns, and the practice song rhythmically punctuating that sleep.

ON A RAZZLE-DAZZLE MAKESHIFT STAGE

I visit a plaza in a newly constructed, pre-planned city.

Perhaps it's due to the war, but every place in Aerok resembles a makeshift stage. Yet this place seems even more so.

The cuboid cement buildings are cloaked with flashing neon signs on every side. No surface remains untouched. The stores in these buildings refuse to compromise, hanging the largest, brightest signs they can afford. In doing so, they overshadow the signage of the stores I seek.

On the first floor of these buildings, there are cosmetics shops, shoe stores, clothing outlets, cell phone stores, and coffee shop chains.

Every brand from Aerok has a presence here.

The 2nd, 3rd, and 4th floors host a variety of restaurants, hospitals, and cafes.

The 5th floor houses a motel,

while the basement is predominantly occupied by karaoke bars.

You could celebrate here continuously, every single day of the year.

Almost all the city's money circulates here, except for what's spent on daily necessities.

The throngs of people crossing the streets bear testimony to a 365-day festival.

The majority of the restaurants and cafes operate 24/7.

Dozens of these cuboid buildings line the streets. What's even more astonishing is that most of those who frequent this temporary stage are under the age of 30. Do they celebrate their fleeting existence with such extravagance? When the glaring lights dim and dawn approaches, the streets resemble the chairs of a restaurant, dripping with filth.

There is no silence here. No darkness. No noble spirit moves through this space. There is no history. It's like a planet illuminated by multiple suns; lights remain on throughout the day and night. Each shop blares its own music, creating an overlapping cacophony of Eastern and Western hits. The buildings, after countless sleepless nights, seem weary. The only remnants of those who've passed through or rooted themselves here are the odd bits of tissue or pools of vomit found each morning. Only that and nothing else, whether you leave or disappear.

There isn't a single tree or book on this street, where both time and 'I' are expended, and eventually squandered. Contemplations don't happen on these streets.
Everyone departs before their 'me' can become 'me.'
The stores, too, frequently relocate. The buildings regularly change their clothes, with the fate of the families linked to these stores hanging in balance. Newer, more razzle-dazzle stores and structures rise in their stead, constructing another makeshift stage.
The streets are littered with toys crafted from a blend of nylon and plastic. Among these toys.
On these streets where no one can settle down. On these streets of endless thirst. Is this the pinnacle of Aerok Civilization, now at its zenith in recorded history?

Then, news of the worst tragedy in Aerok's history swept through this city of the makeshift stages. And amidst these impermanent structures and utility poles, banners of condolences unfurled, mourning the lost lives, juxtaposed with the names of politicians in the throes of election season.

THE FACE OF A QUILT

Sitting on the black living room floor of the centuries-old master house,
As if I am treating my body with good medicine,
I sip on a dark wine within this darkness
When the lady of the house comes to talk to me
Like a ghost whose delightful voice seeps
Into darkness, inviting me to join her for a morning walk
Because there is something I must come and see in the mountain.

Wild and thick grasses, hair-like,
Grow everywhere, begging to be asked why do you live on the mountain.
Now that we are past spring and summer, you will find on mountain paths
Tiny yellow flowers, shaped like rice seedlings, dangling on the mountain's hair.
The mountain is all yellow.
As if a yellow snowstorm had crashed upon the mountain.
In the middle of the night, the lady of the house tries to hook Lady No into going to see that sight.
But Lady No argues with the lady in the darkness that
She is satisfied with this sight that now appears in her mind's eye.

The lady of the house speaks again.
When you change the quilt's cover after someone sleeps in it, you can see them.
The smell changes, and the wrinkles on the fabric are different, too.

Some visitors leave wrinkles as if they drew themselves on the quilt five thousand times.

Some visitors leave no trace as if they never touched the quilt, as if a ghost had slept there.

It is different for each person.

The faces and the bodies of their sleeps are all different.

And though we cannot see them with our eyes, all the yellow snowflowers are different, too.

MOTHERS DESPISE DOING IT TOO

Lady No despises children who claim the tapping of their mother's kitchen knife is their favorite sound in the world. Believing that your mother is happy when she is chopping with her knife is a mistake. She must peel and trim. She must go out to buy those things before she can chop them into pieces. It is tiresome. She never wants to do it. Dirt gets underneath her fingernails. Slippery things get spilled on the floor. When a dish slips out of the fridge, everything spills out, and the dish shatters. All that must be cleaned up. Rags must be laundered. A knife cuts open a hand. If the house isn't dusted off for more than two days, dust runs rampant throughout the house. Lady No despises the song with the lines that go, mother salted a fish and put it in the fridge. Lady No really despises putting her hand inside the mouth of a fish. She also despises the poem in which the speaker professes his love for the round dining table filled with dishes that his mother prepared. Lady No thinks that collective effort may have gone into gaslighting mothers. This life of domestic labor, once you fool yourself into it, there is no way out. Hypnotized by the myth of the mother, you place meat and vegetables on the cutting board and go after them with your knife. After a while, dishes will be glued to your hands, and they won't come off. Mothers dutifully serve this unceasing myth of maternity and suffer the most. Being mothers. Serving the invisible order, tasked to bring prosperity to their offspring every year, mothers give up their lives to make things that will go into someone else's mouth. Sometimes—no, quite often—mothers despise doing it too.

TEARSTAIN GROWTH RINGS

After a night at the master house,
While having breakfast in the inner quarters, the lady of the house approaches again.
Lady No looks at the lady of the house and thinks.
There are so many things this lady wants to do, and so many places she wants to go,
And she wants to leave here for another country,
But how heavy a burden must the life of a daughter-in-law of the master house be?
Opening each lid of those large food jars, how tired she must be at the sight of soybean paste and gochujang.

The lady of the house speaks.
When you can't fall asleep lying on a quilt in the master house by the river on a snowy night,
You can hear the willow trees by the river succumbing to the cold
And howling as they shatter! Shatter! Shatter!
Their sorrow is so great that they are inconsolable. All one can do is to curl up and listen.
After such winter nights pass and spring arrives, willow trees form another growth ring.

Lady No sits still and thinks about a tree with a ring of frozen tearstains wrapped around its body.
About a willow tree loosening her green hair like a spring girl when spring arrives.

After breakfast, she goes down to the river, where skinny willow trees stand in rows

Like the trees drawn on large food jars.

The trees seem to want to pack their belongings and go far away, past fall, past winter.

OH, HONEST POEM!

When her students say that a poem is excellent, Lady No asks them why.

The students answer,

"The poet is being honest. The poet is talking about their experience."

Lady No questions her students again.

"How did you figure out that this poet is being honest?

Could it be that the poet used another's experience and made it their own?

Wouldn't it have been better for the poet to write a memoir instead of a poem?

Which genre is the most unrealistic? Memoir, biography, or history?"

(It may be the case that Lady No can't trust a memoirist who uses their life as their writing's ingredient. Is the content of a memoir the writer's reality, or the writer's hopes?)

In their poems, or memoirs, is it possible that the writer wrapped themselves in the hypocrisy of "I am being honest" as if it were a scarf, and then manipulated a poetic self into being?

(How can anyone make an order out of so many confessions, and then plot out a narrative?)

Lady No keeps questioning.

We question and answer to be nearer to 'poetry.'

Literature is inherently not honest.

Poetry is a lie against the conventional use of language,

and fiction is a lie against the conventional use of reality.

Perhaps, a writer is someone who knows that after we disappear, only our lies will remain.

Poetry is when the poetic speaker forgets they share their body with an ordinary self.

It is when they cut out the intestines of their ordinary self and scatter its smell to the winds.

(Like when a Mongolian nomad's wife slaughters a lamb and scatters the shit from the animal's colon on a tree's branches)

It is when a structure, already built, emerges from underneath the language. But it is also when the structure is immediately destroyed.

It is when the structure embraces the world and then spits it out.

It is when you extend one arm toward a place that is not here.

It is when that arm contracts and deforms after reaching a place that is not here.

Should we not call that poetry?

Instead of being honest, when the poet's sensitivity and the vast cosmos rendezvous.

When life doesn't string together smoothly like links in a chain.

When it feels like meaning has evaporated from our ordinary experience, like mentally exhausted patients returning from their lodgings.

After dragging their dog by the leash, a child sits listlessly by the side of a road, and then sees the world in its entirety. That moment. Like that desolation.

How on earth can we draw a line between what is honest and what is not honest about our sense of self?

To write poetry is to place something that is nothing in the middle of spokes, spinning the machine of oblivion at full speed. Against the judgment of usefulness, it is utterly useless, spinning the absences that can't even be used as ingredients of a story.

RATIONAL NUMBER'S INFINITY

While watching the election night broadcast, Lady No decided that she would only check the score of the candidate she supported. She felt this was the only way for her side to win. Lady No consciously decided against watching the opposition's score. Her candidate's score kept going up, the numbers growing in number. When Lady No turned off her TV screen, she realized that the digital tallies of her candidate's score were now ingrained on one of her irises. Even though the election was over, a board of pictures showing the rising numbers was now installed in one of Lady No's eyes. The score for her candidate rose beyond the number of voters and the number of people living in Aerok. In Lady No's eye, the election night broadcast didn't end. And it took a long time to turn it off.

He had written countless books. He had written the history of torture in Aerok. All night, Lady No read his books, and in the morning, she opened the window of her veranda and looked down at the unchanging streets and sang a song. "Even in a dream, how can we ever forget that land." By singing, Lady No scrubbed herself to wash off the unceasing screams that had come from the records of heinous tortures she had read. She did this so that she could go to school. She had to wash off everything she had read the night before. To face her fresh students in broad daylight, who were coming to school with new song compositions, Lady No had to.

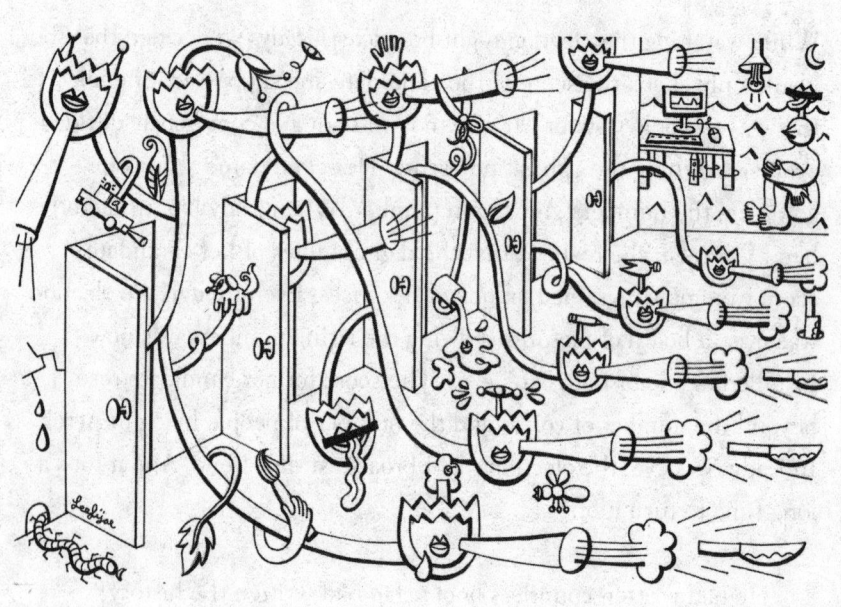

FLOWERS OF THE WORLD

After getting all packed for moving, my teacher's belongings came down the aerial ladder.
They didn't stop coming down.
A wardrobe and a television,
A refrigerator and a laundry machine,
A desk and bookshelves,
They all came down
And then something else came down again endlessly.
How could there have been space for all those things in that small house for forty years?
So much came down without an end that my question rose up.
One moving truck left after being filled up.
Then the second truck left.
Then the third truck left.
Then the fourth truck left.
My teacher arrived at his new house and unpacked alone because his wife was sick.
He unpacked and unpacked but there was still more to unpack.
The new house was soon full of dishes.
The dishes were filled with weird shapes and colors, stacking up endlessly.
The dishes had been collected for 40 years
And they had never been plated with food
And they had come from England, Spain, Italy, and China
And they kept spilling over.
The dishes could fill up the new house and there would still be more left.
The dishes kept coming out of unpacked boxes.

They were unstacked on the floor until no one could stand on the floor.

My teacher screamed and
His wife laughed.
My teacher suffered and
His wife buried herself in happiness.
Dish flowers blossomed inside the house.
A flower field blossomed until it spilled over.

THE SONG OF AN EMPTY ROOM

There was a singer who, though not particularly skilled at singing, had an uncanny ability to sink into the pit of your stomach. His lyrics were akin to singing prose, his voice imbued with innocence, full of life, possessed with an eternal tremble. His singing style was such that even if one tried to hold onto his song, it felt as though it were far away. He died a few days short of living as long as Jesus.

Lady No often listened to his songs. She listened to them again and again until her mouth tasted salty just from listening. She pondered why she listened so often, and realized it was because whenever he sang, his or someone else's songs, his voice made the tremble buried in those songs tremble for the first time, resonating deeply in her heart. While listening to his songs, she felt ashamed of growing older than him.

In one television program, they concealed people behind curtains who were exceptional at imitating someone else's singing voice and had them compete against him. The audience was tasked with identifying the fake voices first and then selecting his true voice. After singing a verse or two, curtains were lifted to reveal small rooms occupied by the imitators, who then emerged onto the stage. However, he did not appear. From his vacant room, only his voice emanated. His room was as clean as clean dirt.

His empty room was immaculate. It was infinite. It embarrassed us. It was anonymous. It was flawless.

Lady No envied this room, as empty as a devoured walnut shell. She was jealous of the one for whom only the voice remained. Perhaps Lady No aspired to be without a body, to be only a voice. The place from which he sang was invisible, a place without a place. His song that slots perfectly into the frame of absence.

RAIN OF POEMS

A helicopter flew above Jubilee Gardens in London. Since early evening, a large crowd had been waiting for the helicopter to arrive. Organized by a Chilean and produced by a German and a Brit, it was a performance made possible by a specially issued license from the city. The event was titled 'Rain of Poems.' Around 9 o'clock, as the sun set, a helicopter appeared in the cloudy sky like a birthmark. It began to drop poems. Not seeds, but poems. They were dropping poems written by poets from all the countries in the world, translated into English, printed on twenty thousand recycled papers. Hundreds of people raised their arms and ran around, trying to catch the poems that were falling like square snowflakes. After securing a few pieces, they stuffed them into their pockets and bags. They laughed and shouted. Some poems left Jubilee Gardens and flew far away, falling into the Thames, landing on pleasure boats, settling on nearby buildings, flying toward Big Ben. Lady No was slow and did not manage to catch any. But a certain man picked up one of the poems and gave it to her, mentioning that it was a poem by a poet from his homeland. "Please feel how good this poem is," he asked her. The helicopter departed, and she was walking through the darkened streets when the poems that had fallen on rooftops began to fly about again. Even though many minutes had passed, people were finally getting around to raising their arms and chasing what was falling from the air. And someone asked her what was happening, why they were doing this. A woman stood disappointed because she hadn't received a single poem, and Lady No gave her the poem that she had received. The woman loudly read the poem on that street. She imagined an incredible vision of a helicopter of Aerok flying above Aerok's Seoul and dropping the ethereal poems written by the poets of the world, translated into the Aerok language. A vision of the people of Aerok running around with their hands lifted, reaching for the poems falling from the sky, as if it were a festival.

LIKE TWO PLANETS IN LOVE

What is distant is beautiful.
Even without envy, it is beautiful,
Like an aged monk and a young disciple atop a towering mountain.

Perhaps we should say what is beautiful isn't the distance, but your ability to perceive the distant.

At sunset, the blue-black silhouettes of two figures stand on a remote mountaintop; they could be arguing. However, viewed from afar, they appear beautiful.
Many things lose their beauty upon closer inspection.
Gazing at something through a convex mirror can make the familiar grotesque, akin to observing microorganisms dwelling in pores.
There are moments when closeness is beautiful, especially when love is involved.
This is when love is blossoming, when I am yet to fully decipher the text that is you.
Perhaps love is viewing something close as though it were distant,
Like maintaining a gap between us as vast as the space between two planets,
Akin to a virus compelling us to observe each other while preserving our distance.
Maybe to see something from afar, the 'death' of 'me'—my 'extinction'—is a prerequisite.
Perhaps love is the journey 'I' undertake to reach and die before you.
Because love is distant, and happiness is near, perhaps destruction is always on the horizon.

When the distant spreads out and reaches me, it is beautiful,
As fragrant as a winter night filled with thoughts of spring arriving at a far-off harbor.

What is distant appears small. Its smallness evokes pity. It might be barely visible. Even invisible, which therefore makes it beautiful. Near yet distant. Loud yet hushed. That which is warm yet frigid. Love's law of perspective.

POETRY WORKSHOP

Constantly getting questions about how teaching poetry writing can be possible,

Thus answers Lady No.

Rather than teaching, there are things we can think about together, and there are things one needs to think about alone. So, Lady No divides and shares with Lady No's students what we should be thinking about together.

Sometimes, suddenly looking all serious, someone asks her, 'What is poetry?'

(But, if the answer to such a question makes poetry subordinate to the development of philosophy, one might bring up the impossibility of the question itself.)

Then, Lady No answers that there are five hundred answers to the question of 'what is poetry?' and those five hundred answers are applied to each specific moment. On top of that, places, feelings, listeners, and the weather make the answers more numerous still.

If the answer to what is poetry cannot be set into a standardized textbook definition, then different answers might be possible for each individual poem. In poetry, a certain truth can be valid, and certain other truths can be invalid. In such cases, poetry is something that cannot be taught or learned.

But if a poem has come out into the world, then there is an answer to 'what is poetry?' that befits a poem in this world. The definition of poetry is endlessly given case-by-case, but the Great Republic of Poetry can never be escaped—perhaps the answer can only be given as an oxymoron.

Like how each of us is born on a specific hour, date, month, and year, giving us the eight characters determining our fate, carrying our individual universes within us as we live—like how we think of the positions of stars as our destiny, in poetry criticism or in poetry workshops, we share the universes that apply independently to each poem—we share the existence of the poet.

So, yesterday, one might have said that the poem is the fruit of inspiration. And then, today, one might ask, What even is an inspiration? Where does it hide before coming to us?

Therefore, poetry is not really something you teach or learn, but it is like coming up with different definitions of poetry while considering different poems every moment. Declaring the uniqueness and singularity of the experience of each poem. Until we arrive at the vast loneliness of poetry every time.

COOKING VERB

Below, please draw a line and connect the Aerok verbs used for cooking to following categories: weather-cooking verbs, heart-cooking verbs, hair-cooking verbs, people-cooking verbs, and language-cooking verbs.

Language	Roasted
	Boiled
Weather	Blanched
	Stir-fried
Heart	Seared
	Brewed
Hair	Poached
	Heated
People	Burnt
	(Vaguely) Mixed
	Steamed

THE INFINITE ACCELERATOR OF ANXIOUS UNIVERSE

It is incredibly easy for Lady No to create a universe that exists solely for Lady No.

Even before Lady No questions her anxiety, a universe adorned with electric stars emerges within the heart of Lady No.

Like squid fishing boats viewed from a marooned spaceship, the electric stars gleam brightly.

The body of Lady No recognizes, like an intuitive understanding, that Earth is a star afloat in space, and her feet begin to tingle. Questioning Lady No's anxiety is akin to questioning the necessity of the universe's existence. There's no answer.

Anxiety, therefore, isn't a state we elect to have or avoid; it's as innate as the universe within and around us. Anxiety doesn't submerge the soul but inhabits the heart, where the electric radiance ceaselessly detonates. The electrical lights dash across the globe as they flicker into existence.

Anxiety, thus, forms the horizon, the bedrock of all other emotions.

A landscape exists within us that we fail to recognize.

It morphs into our past, either weightlessly soaring or submerging into the black, blurry abyss of time, but it remains real. It is a landscape etched by pain that penetrates the bones, a disarray of emotions and thoughts of Lady No, all jumbled in chaos.

We are filled with the echoes of stars we've bypassed.
We are teeming with shadows of pain we've traversed.
They are shrieking with cries we can't decipher.
They are ablaze and frozen like stone.
Stars that hover in the fathomless expanse of space, whirling in madness and boredom.

From the bottomless bottom of Lady No, floating particles of angst rise, defining the now of Lady No.

Feeding anxiety into the infinite accelerator and initiating the process causes the planet of emotions to expand from within Lady No. Then, the desk of Lady No, books of Lady No, and body of Lady No whirl and get pulled into the vortex.

Like an event unfolding in a dream, an unstable, will-less universe, trembling from vertigo, expands.

Infinite skies, vast and boundless, the expanding universe. Stars of anxiety gleaming, illuminating.

A communion unfolds between the anxiety of God and the anxiety of Lady No.

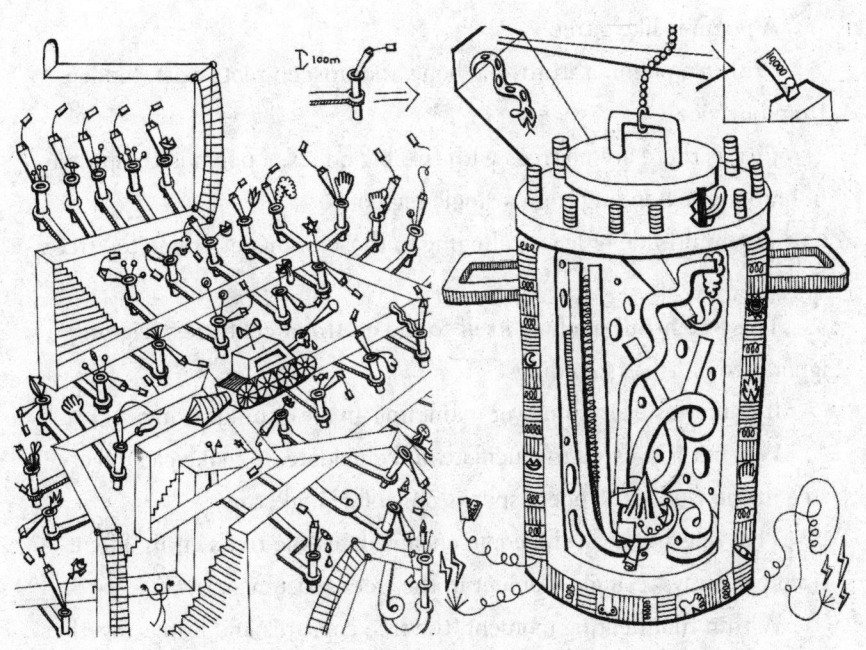

A POEM IS A TREE

A poem is like a tree.

Within a poem, a sturdy big bone and unseen roots exist, hidden from our view.

Just as there are no trees with two big bones, a poem is composed of branches extending from a single big bone.

The multitude of leaves clinging to those branches create the tree's texture.

The tree firmly anchors itself to the earth for centuries, feigning ignorance of its surroundings.

It perceives everything yet maintains an air of unknowing.

When it is pressed to elucidate and elucidate, to make clear every tree in the world, the poem speaks only of a single tree.

That doesn't mean the poem encapsulates the tree's entire life; it simply portrays a single moment in the tree's existence.

Within that fleeting moment, the tree captures and brings together all the trees of the world.

The poem isolates the world as if it were a tree.

Naturally, in that instant, it seems as though the tree is the only living thing in the world.

UNDERGROUND LONELINESS

The pre-recorded broadcasting system for the subway might have broken.
The live voice of the conductor vibrated through the cars.

"Next station is Dongjak Station.
The door is on your left.
The doors are closing."

On each broadcast, the conductor used a different rhythm for each station, as if he were performing steps of a dance with his tongue.
The riders who heard him giggled a little.

At the next station, he used yet another rhythm to say, "The doors are closing."
The riders waited, closely listening to him, wondering what kind of speech pattern would be used to announce, "The doors are closing."
The emotion that was carried on the accents, speed, beat, and pronunciation of those syllables divided into an infinite sequence and rang through the cars.

Every time he performed his "The doors are closing" routine, his loneliness in the underground tunnels was piercingly delivered to each rider's heart. Each rider was bound to find their station and leave his train, but he would return and pass through this place again in time.
So, we had no choice but to giggle a little.

Once, I saw a camera that was installed right next to the train conductor.

It was during the days of the subway workers' union strikes.

The train's engine car was pulling ten cars into the darkness, and for the conductor, the 'next station' was the world of light.

His life was the repetition of darkness and light hundreds of times each day.

Platforms appeared and disappeared again and again, like they would to the brain of someone seeing hallucinations. The hours of the cave spinning endlessly while carrying hundreds of people.

And then, coming above ground on the rails was a momentary whiteout, like going into the bright tunnel that the dead go into.

And that is how the conductors sit in the same spot for decades, repeating through the sequence of bright stations and dark tunnels.

They experience our night and day many hundreds of times in a single day.

And on the weekends, they probably do their grocery shopping or grab a hold of a television remote.

One evening, the doors kept closing.

Whenever the doors closed, there was a different announcement.

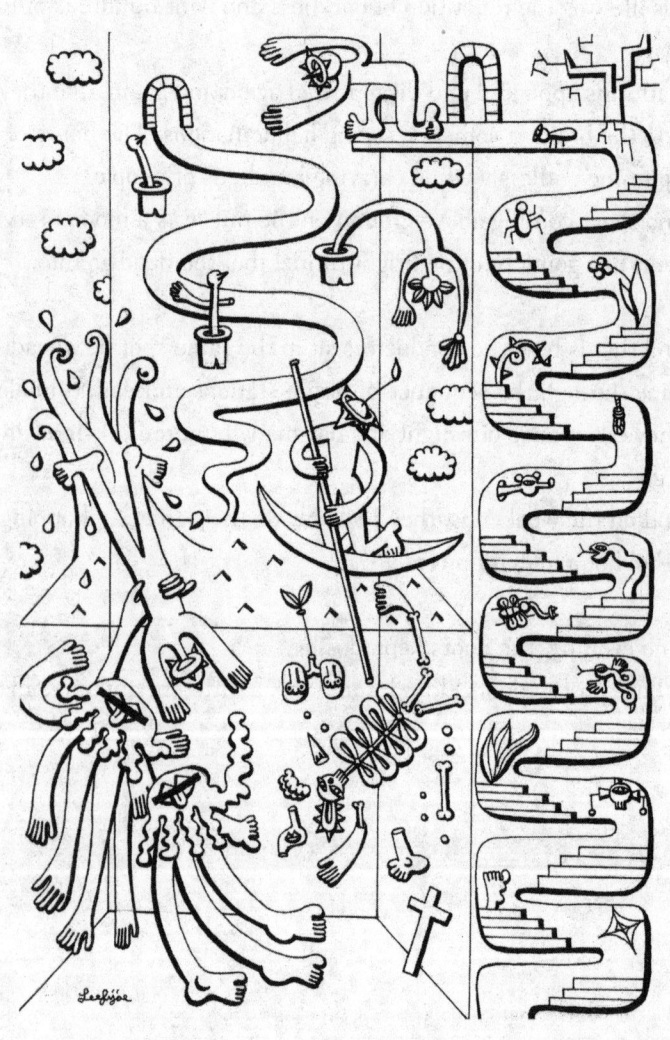

MANHOLE HUMANITY

Lady No imagines.
People bearing manhole covers atop their heads.

Sewers flowing beneath the feet of those seated at the table.
The moment they leave the body, they head straight to the sewers, things that had once been the body itself.

Though we differ in form and differ in hue and differ in personalities,
Beneath, a network of sewage channels links our entrails.

There, where we flow in all at once.
There, where we flow in all as one.

An unconditional and infinite abyss of darkness, without start or finish.
The pitiful and endless cycle of our backs turned away.

We gently seal that place with manhole covers,
And with napkins placed on our knees, we eat our dinner.

Saying, it isn't the hour.
Saying, it isn't the hour to think about it yet.

Saying, our only task is to keep the covers firmly in place.
With filthy, terrifying waste beneath our feet, like a sewer rat listening to the cries of a cat living downstairs.

In the end, our lower bodies will be connected by that dreary blackness,

But for now, let's believe our wounds, which crash-landed on us, keep their lips sealed. Their hour hasn't come yet.

Lady No quietly presses her manhole cover down onto her head.

A future excrement known as Lady No hasn't yet reached the sewerage treatment facility.

EMPTY FRAME

The oldest wooden building in Aerok is a black Buddhist temple.

When she arrived at the temple, she came upon a memorial service, a rite performed three days after the day of death.

The sorrowful chanting of the sutras echoed all the way toward the temple's main gate.

A monk chanting the sutras.

A monk rapping on a moktak.

A monk holding a washbasin.

A monk with their neck dressed in bandage.

The monks led the procession in a single file, followed by someone in a leather jacket carrying a large bundle, followed by a family member, withered from their sorrow, holding a frame.

Inside the frame was a portrait of a young woman, who had a face you might encounter in the markets, the streets, and the stalls.

Curly permed hair, red vinyl jacket.

Inside the frame was a face of a woman whose cheeks were turning rosy in a heated room after coming in from the cold.

The procession trailed toward a brazier, which looked like a stone lantern, below the temple.

Lady No followed them.

When their chanting was done, the bundle of dead girl's clothes was entered into the brazier's flame.

White skirts, jackets, and rubber shoes of mourners entered the flame.

And the last thing to enter the flame was her portrait from the frame.

The frame, now empty, did not enter the flame.
The smoke rose above the chimney.
Her face was set on fire. It was now grey smoke.
Only the empty frame remained.
The glass that had covered the photograph remained, too.
The place where her face once remained without her.
Now 'her absence' entered her frame.

The youngest monk collected the frame.
A blank sheet of paper left inside the frame flashed once.

ARRIVING AT A FORM

Lady No's time is a dream dreamt by Lady No's death.

Poetry is the discovery of a form that deconstructs this dream.

A poetic subjectivity's work is to go beyond death's content, a movement that erects the form.

A structure of the moment built outside of time. A poetic speaker's rhythm bringing tension to the structure.

It neither pierces nor transcends the content, for it is a multidimensional map in the form of a hidden weeping. (Therefore, the best reader deciphers each poem's map of bones, which is made from the weeping that is specific to each piece.) Following a thread spun from a thin yet taut voice—perhaps even an invisible one—will likely reveal the sudden emergence of a poem's beauty.

Every time a poem is written, what happens isn't the renewed inventions of dreams and perceptions, nor the manifestations of existence, instead

It is something that supports the muscles, allowing them to flow like a river where they are inseparably intertwined, like fabric brimming with patterns.

Believing that this ugly reality, this reality of sameness that continues day after day, this reality that comes for us all, will be atoned.

Poetry is when the sad wounded things, and the things that do not exist yet, come together within a form, through which thinking rises.

Speaking in reverse, it is a frame breathing within various grains.

The thinking subject flows along the poetic framework.

All the literary content of the world is imperfect, and this can't be helped. They are incomplete and secret. Their incomplete secrets are embraced by the invisible frame called form.

In that moment of embrace, the text becomes a singular space. Where loneliness and ennui flow like fog, where war bleeds and emptiness screams, where madness flows like a ghost, where death soars, where joy chirps, where grief becomes as pathetic as a dinner table for one, where waves run across the sky, where silence burns like a wounded breast, where the voice of light is heard, it becomes a non-place, carried away by the beauty and fear bestowed by death.

Therefore, form is an orchestration sewn using those steely veins that remain after a steel mesh scrubber's layers wore off from use.

Form of thin veins appearing after trees' leaves greenery wears off. Form of a musical score through which trees' branches radiate outward. Like humidity that manifests itself as a morning dew on leaves which yet remains invisible as it spreads out into the air.

Blood veins all over a piece of liver. Like neural pathways of a brain, like lines on your palm.

Not a content of desperation or howling

But the form of that desperation!

It is felt the moment the first breath leaves the body.

The pulse that beats regardless of there being a meaning, the unidentified flying object's engine leaving for the grand freedom, our home.

And yet, it is a blueprint for reaching nothingness! Inside a steel mesh scrubber fruit, its steely veins are thin and tough like fishing lines, and they weave rooms around an emptiness at the scrubber's center, and that is the same as how

The whirlwind of the poetic world radiates outward infinitely, while keeping the nothingness at the center of its centrifugal and centripetal forces.

Within that place, because it is forgotten endlessly, a poetic consciousness exists, trembling in its longing.

A beauty trembling to extinction. The reader striker.

But the kind of poetry that seeks to win over large readership is different.

It is not a form but a content, the ceaseless sentimental overflow of a poetic consciousness, aphorisms of soundbites providing immediate satisfaction. The all-too-common poetic speaker's grief and sentiment. The disguised sanctity emanating from there, but once uncovered, it is nothing more than flesh trembling in unbearable narcissism.

The vanity that is called innocence.

PONTIUS PILATE GOVERNORS

When I am interviewing applicants or judging a contest, I feel like I have become Pontius Pilate.

I must choose someone, and I must reject others.

I hold in my hands the absolute power of life and death.

I bombard trembling interviewees with questions.

I say to the crying interviewee, pretending to be kind, that they need to answer the question in their allotted time

But I am just trying to get it over with.

Choosing people, rejecting people,
Sentencing people,
Judging events,
These Pontius Pilates.
People who keep going higher.
People who have worn, are wearing, or are trying to wear black robes.
People who try to judge anything
Will have their names listed somewhere
Just as it is written somewhere that "He was sentenced to death by Pontius Pilate."

Indecisive judges who
Don't know they will be judged in the end
Believing their standards of judgment are the most rational and right
Are giving scores,
Are handing out sentences,
Are choosing and rejecting.

When selecting someone,
It feels as though I've inevitably approached the final judgment seat.

This year, people of Aerok all felt this, this feeling of being an adult who judges.
It felt like placing a name on the list of murderers and bystanders.
It felt like the day of judgment was at hand.
Knowing this, we still judge, and we choose.

NIGHTMARE SOUP

In the west of Ying County in Shanxi, the oldest octagonal wooden pagoda in the world still stands. It is a great pagoda. For many generations, the Huns kept invading this region, killing many of its people. The wooden pagoda was built in response in 1056 CE. Within the pagoda, numerous clay-sculpted buddhas sit in a circle, and a circular hallway surrounds these buddhas. This layout allows the visitors to either pray to the clay buddhas or look down at the town below. Long time ago, when Lady No visited this structure for the first time, the pagoda was in disrepair, and it wasn't being restored. It wasn't even being managed. From a distance, the painted pagoda looked black because of the swallows. When I got nearer, the chaos was visible, and it seemed like arrows and swords of soldiers numbering in tens of thousands were clashing. The swallows had built their nests on the walls and the roofs of this pagoda, and they were bringing food for their babies. Instead of the pagoda itself, I was more curious about how all those swallows would find their way home in that chaos. The swallows were relentlessly slapping the great pagoda. In each of its five floors, the clay buddhas, proudly displaying their sitting heights, were fading, losing their painted colors. They had lost parts of their flesh and seemed to be dressed in rags. When I reached the pagoda's top, at least the sky was blue, opening like a blue fan, giving current to the wind. However, after leaving the pagoda and reaching the town below, my nightmare deepened when I arrived at a place known as restroom. The content of the restroom flowed out beyond the restroom's floor and spilled over into the streets. It was impossible to tell the restroom apart from what was outside of it, but people kept taking shit. And beside the shit takers, their neighbors were slurping noodles. I wanted to forget what I saw as quickly as I could, but I couldn't.

SYLVIA AND MRS. BROWN'S BREAD

In the movie *Sylvia*, Sylvia bakes bread. Ted returns from his walk and writes poetry again and again, but Sylvia stacks her breads high above their table. Apparently, Sylvia thinks her husband is sacrilegious for stealing the words of the ocean and nature from outside their home. Sylvia seems to suffer from the duality of hatred and astonishment when it comes to her feelings for Ted. Ted chastises Sylvia for baking instead of writing poetry, but she is ceaseless in her bread-baking in her kitchen in their solitary house in the great view of the ocean. The poetry of the ocean, its tides breaking grandly in silver light, and the breads baked with flour dough made with her arms' force. Poetry and bread. Poetry and the ocean. Beside him, the bread looks shabby and mean, like the ordinary next to great nature. Ted steals from nature, but Sylvia opens her inner eye and steals from what is there, so it can't be helped her poetry will always seem so. I think Ted and Sylvia's poetry could be compared this way, too.

In Sylvia Plath's poem "Lesbos," the speaker of the poem, who has given birth to her babies, is in the kitchen. Her cat and babies' excrement fill the air with terrible smell, and the pussycat vomits, and her husband rolls on the floor coiled in his chains, and her infant is wailing, and Sylvia's nerves are shredded. Sylvia lets out her wrath-filled scream through her poetry, but how many people heard her?

A few years after Sylvia killed herself, why did Assia Wevill, who began a relationship with Ted while Sylvia was still alive, also kill herself in the same way, even after surviving the Holocaust? She took her child with her, too. Why did they all die in the kitchen? After much time had passed, why did Ted blame Assia and call her "the dark power that destroyed Sylvia" and shirk his responsibility to her? What did Ted ever understand, and what could he never know even to his death?

In the movie *The Hours*, Mrs. Brown prepares for her husband's birthday with her son's help. She spreads flour and bakes a chocolate cake. After finishing her cake, she throws it away in a trash can, then checks into a hotel room all alone. Curled up like a small ball on a big hotel mattress, she reads *Mrs. Dalloway*. Laboring away in the kitchen is about making things that will go on the top of someone else's tongue, performed with movements that will repeat endlessly once one falls into them, a formless labor that repeats itself every day. The cake is the chosen one, the symbol of those hours that pass, a false ritual that pretends to be reimbursed with astonishment and praise. Household structure makes it impossible not to feel that on the other side of all this cake-baking, someone is eating it for free (do you understand? O people outside of the kitchen!). And so, the mother's inner destruction infects her children. And later, Mrs. Brown's son kills himself.

Scenes of dishes made from the kitchen being placed on a clean table every day, and then the scenes of them being eaten. Somehow, sad.

AN ASPIRING FICTION WRITER

An aspiring fiction writer came and talked to Lady No.
"I promise I will become a famous fiction writer."
Lady No asks him a question.
"Do you at least have a role model?"
The student answers.
"I don't have such a writer, but I have a composite of many writers that is my role model.
I will wake up every morning and write my novel like a laborer.
I will start my novel while drinking coffee."
"Okay, so what kind of novel do you want to write?"
Lady No asked him again.
"I don't know yet, but I can see how my back will look when I sit down to write my novel.
I can see my novel that's been published.
I promise to be a writer."
"You do you," Lady No answers.
But Lady No thinks.
Even if you write a novel, most of the time publishers reject it.
And after feeling like you wasted your life on a single novel, you start looking for a part-time job or learn a trade, until you get a call from some magazine.
But that doesn't lead anywhere.
No one comes to you with a query. You submit endlessly to magazines.
So, you publish a few stories.
And finally, you get your book to come out from a publisher.
You are unsatisfied with it, so you want to trash every copy, but you calm yourself.

However, there isn't even a single line of review, not even a bad review.

And then another round of mental issues, loneliness, and servility. Lady No asks.

"The endless void and the encounter with your voice that comes back to you without ever making an echo, do you know about this path of writers?

You really want to go on that path?"

THE NAMES OF SARDINES AND MALLARDS

After the graduates leave, the first-years arrive. The life of a teacher moves in accordance with this cycle. After the graduates leave school, the space between their names and faces grows. Sometimes, the teacher encounters a face and thinks, 'that is one of my graduates', but their name will take too long to come back to the teacher's mind, or it may never come back at all. However, most faces never grow distant. The impression of a face stays somewhere in our brainstems until they explode at the moment of an encounter, and their memories flood back. But there are faces and names that can never be forgotten. It is not because they write well, or because they did bad things, or because they shared a memorable episode with the teacher, yet their faces and names remain in our minds forever. Sometimes, they even make appearances in our dreams. It is impossible to know why their memories remain with us in such a pristine manner.

This is the order in which a memory disappears:
First, the name falls off from a face.
And a personal pronoun takes that place.
A truly long roundabout way must be traveled before a name and a person can be glued together to be pronounced together.
One may have to take a train to Busan just to know a graduate's name.

Next, names and objects fall away from one another.
Verbs turned into nouns take their places.
For instance, a spoon should really be called 'a thing that you move from a bowl to your mouth when you are having soup.'

Adjectives disappear next.

You forget that there is a world expressed by adjectives.

All you have left is to drown in the mirages of your sorrows, fears, and pains.

A formless, colorless mass remains before a person from whom personal pronouns and common nouns have disappeared.

An object that was once defined by its noun begins to expand toward borderless infinity.

Only a colorless stillness that needs no parts of speech remains, and it is like a poor stillness surrounding a tiny pebble that hasn't yet turned into a pearl.

Within a family of sardines swimming in the shape of a large ball in the water, and within a flock of mallards flying up and down a reservoir, a singular being becomes aware of their singular sensations and perceives each individual movement within their groups, feeling sadness and happiness, and for some reason, the sight of their awareness is sorrowful. And if they are also aware of each object's singularity, then that is a cause for even greater sorrow. However, an ability to differentiate shape and essence from these singularities will grow, and a syntactic ability to recognize the value of a part will grow, too.

And when we reverse this process, we can draw the map of oblivion. The soot of oblivion steals names from people and objects, and steals their boundaries, and leaves behind inexpressible vestiges. Such is the order. The order of how a human returns to nature. The order of how a human sinks into nature's operation.

Therefore, obliviating is a step in the process of transference from object to energy.

For instance, a rose blossoms. But only blossoms, blossoms, and blossoms linger. It feels like the name of the flower could be somewhere else, so one looks for it by flipping through a dictionary or calls someone up and asks them. A single rose blossoming in darkness, but it cannot be pulled out from behind one's lips. Then suddenly, before one's eyes, a rose blossoms in the light of the sun, and shines. And then, one speaks loudly, 'rose blossoms,' as if they are saying the words for the first time after being born. As if one is revealing a poem, as if one is naming a name for the first time. And yet, in this universe, outside of this universe, there are things like our pain, things not yet given their syntactic value, that are both visible and invisible, crowding up the space, that have not yet been named. Like how in the swimming school of sardines, within that ball of them, one beautiful sardine is.

TO MY MIND

If I ever get hold of you, then I will pierce your loose earlobes and grace them with a pair of golden bells. Next, I will place a golden necklace around your neck as if it is engagement day for puppies, and I will drape lace with cloud patterns over your shoulders. I will decorate your wrists with noisy golden bracelets, and I will chain your ankles with a golden chain. If I can grab hold of you, the terrifying you, then I will tie endlessly bursting fireworks to your tail. I will tag your forehead with a fluorescent name tag and embed a golden piercing into your belly button. I will blow my mouth's breath into your anus and inflate you bigger than the cumulus clouds above the mountain before my house. And then, I will march with you proudly for everyone in our village to see. I will use beautiful flowers as ticklers to tickle your backs and butts when we come home. Next, I will make you worship yourself at the sanctum where you lie on your side because of how big you are. I will make you prostrate yourself three times, and I will cut strands of your hair to burn as incense, and I will show you your teeth capped with gold, and I will show your face remade from dust that I made from grinding down your bones, and since those things are flesh and blood, we will share them and feast on them and drink them up, and I will never say such things, and I will never really say such things. But only this, at daybreak when no one is awake, I will cast you out, and as you run for your life after finally being cast out, I will clap and laugh loudly and bid you farewell. And when you've become a beggar, I will never spare a change.

AUGUST

PIANO AND CAMEL

If, even after many days and nights, even after many months and years, there is music that does not end.

If someone is playing a song that will erase 'me' when the music finishes.

If 'I' am living in music that is already composed.

If the scale and rhythm of the music's prelude is where 'my' flesh and blood come from.

And if the music is an invisible cloth that 'I' am always clothed in,

And an old camel crossing the desert to the music is what keeps Lady No's time.

If the camel's knees are bending.

The sound of piano keys being pressed, drawing near like tinnitus,

And inside the piano is a terrifying, wind-swept world.

In there, the subjects pass by carrying gems and sulfur, and

Sandstorms blow, and

Poplar trees of an oasis shudder.

If the hot days and cold nights are already being composed like the sailing logs of the planet Earth.

The sleeves of the pianist should be rotting away now, but

The wind rises and climbs up against the flow of fingers. 'My' calendar's December 31st, midnight.

If the camel caught inside the sand is howling.

If the pianist is already playing after imprisoning 'me' inside longing.

REVOLUTIONARY'S NEW JOB

It must be hard for a revolutionary to get a job after revolution.

Can being a revolutionary be a job.

Among ex-revolutionaries of Aerok (specifically literature majors), three job categories are most noticeable.

The first being those who became lawmakers.
The second being those who became poets who write love poems.
The third being those who became tourists.
(Of course, there are also social activists, farmers, mental patients, publishers, professors, teachers, still-somehow-writers, real estate moguls, still-somehow-revolutionaries, and so on and so forth, many who have managed to get new careers, and many who are keeping true to the revolutionary struggle in their daily lives and jobs, and many who have passed away, but the ex-revolutionaries who are most noticeable to us now belong to the three aforementioned categories.)

And in those categories, there are those who work as all three, or just two, but rarely just one. Among them, the ones who write love poems write such poems with religious connotations, but they are never sensual nor pornographic. They despise and call grotesque the pornographic poets and the young poets who howl about failures. From the perspective of Lady No, this is because they still see poetry as a tool for the revolution of romantic enlightenment. The types who became tourists like to take photos as well, but they don't go to Africa, Europe, or North America. They only go to places in Asia. The themes of their travels are about healing, reconciliation, and mutual understanding. The usual sentiment behind their lenses is nostalgia.

They console themselves with landscapes they think are less civilized. To prove that revolutionaries are human beings after all, Lady No thinks that these people should get a better second job by starting pornographic scandals or going to camera-restricted areas in New York, London, and/or Tokyo and try to put their lenses on folks there and get their asses beaten. This isn't something someone who enjoys the benefits of their revolution should say or think, but Lady No hates how the ex-revolutionaries find a poor country and take photos of people there who are beyond humble that they don't even try to show any self-consciousness. Somehow the ex-revolutionaries must miss our country's past.

SELF-APPOINTED MEASUREMENT STANDARD OF ALL CREATION

A first-year asks.

I have no idea what this is saying, teacher, how can you tell us this work is good when it reads like utter nonsense like ghosts shelling millet. Do you actually understand what it is?

The first-year is angry.

Benjamin said, "Unrefined masses are caught in the insane anger toward the life of the mind." He also said in a sneer, "Those people line up and march into the department store like they are charging into a concentrated gunfire." He continued, "To read what is not written is the true reading."

Such angry people lurk everywhere. They are the self-appointed measurement standards of all creation.

They do not try to feel, and they do not try to understand, but only put forward their emotions.

They are particularly generous to difficult art or music, but they get angry at difficult literature.

Who can understand this work?

Perhaps that work did not wish to be understood. It could be that it only wanted you to feel it. It could be that it only wanted you to look at it.

But perhaps the measurement standards think that language should only be focused on transference of information and creation of relationships. Perhaps that's why they get angry if language is used to draw an image or explore the world of sounds. Perhaps they refuse to accept that language has aesthetic abilities. Perhaps they do not want to encounter an unfamiliar world drawn up by language.

Sizes of people who come to look at a work are all different.

Each brings with them an appropriately sized dish to hold whatever they can manage to perceive. The shapes are all different, too.

One person brings with them a spoon.

Another brings with them a bathtub, and another brings with them an emptied ocean.

Another brings with them a roentgen.

People with smaller dishes tend to be more angry.

Isn't this all a bunch of nonsense? I don't get it?

They say it is violence when their spoon can't scoop up the work.

But for the writer, those who come with spoons are the violence.

Poets can know the size of the people who come to meet their works.

From their questions, from their silences, and from their expressions,

Whether they feel, whether they find the meaning, or whether they are stuck to their ways.

Poets can measure the approximate size of their dishes.

A poet carries the weight of their readers' misunderstandings like a person without a home pushing all their belongings on a cart.

The size of the work is not decided by the size of the people who come to meet the work.

The work is good when its infinite abilities can expand and contract its own size in infinite measure.

The more deeply felt and expressed can end up weaker in its delivery.

A work where everyone brings the same dish and measures the same size is so-so.

The Famous and The Obscure

There are famous people and obscure people in the world. Among the obscure, there are those who would like to be famous, and there are those who are not concerned. And among the unconcerned, there are those who would like to get involved, and there are those who would hide. Among those who would hide, there are those who are hidden, and those who remain unseen though they didn't try to hide. Among those who like to hide, there are those who want to save humankind in ways that normal people can't see, and there are those who aren't interested in saving anyone but themselves. And there are those who are hard at work saving themselves, and there are those who tried hard to save themselves but gave up. I walked past the houses of monks who voluntarily imprisoned themselves in prayer, but for some reason, I knew that they were sitting inside, listening closely to the footsteps of Lady No.

Attention from others, delight from others, they are baggage. They are restrictions.

The most famous person is the least free.

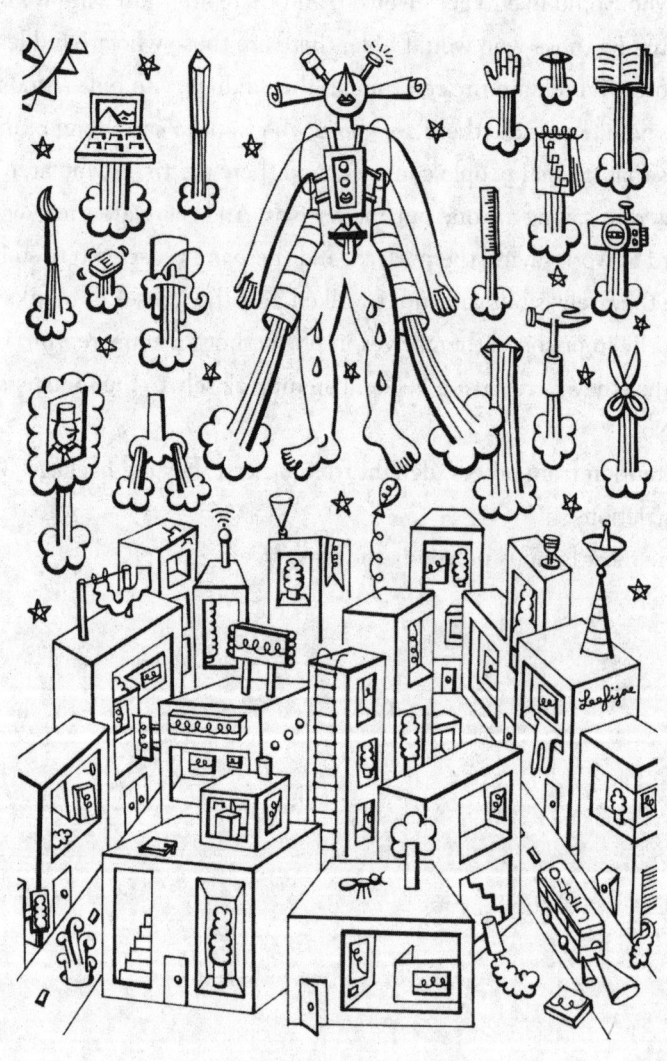

WAITING FOR MY VERY OWN GIRAFFE

I take a giraffe out with me and head to work.
The giraffe always likes to sit next to me.
I take a giraffe out with me to grab a meal.
I take a giraffe out with me and offer it a drink.
"Sorry, but I'll go alone this time," I say,
leaving the giraffe seated on a chair
while I head to the restroom.

After losing the giraffe tonight,
I sit by the door of my house and wait for its return.
The lost giraffe's neck is longer than the giraffe that wasn't lost.

It is a secret that I live with the giraffe, and that is why
I cannot file a missing person's report or
Shout, "O Giraffe! O Giraffe!"

Do you think when death nears, a giraffe will also look for a place to hide on its own?
But its neck is so long it will be seen from everywhere.
Waiting for my giraffe tonight, my neck grows long.

Walking with the giraffe made loneliness go away.
Lying down with the giraffe, I didn't feel so desolate.

I couldn't even close the coffin lid.
Its long neck stuck out past the edges.

Where is the giraffe hanging out this late at night?
Did it go to the meadow all by its lonesome?

With my two arms, meant to fling open the front door, stuck into its head,
    where could it possibly be walking to?

A SONG THAT CAME AND WENT AS A HUM

From outside the office, a lively tune without lyrics briefly drifted in.

Short and barely audible, but the melody was clear.

The sound carried Lady No to a faraway place.

For a moment, Lady No stayed in this weird position where she existed both at a distant place of high altitude and beside this low place of the window.

That short sound made Lady No into a being who was both outside and inside the window.

She clasped her hands because she feared that both could disappear if she opened her window.

A song that sounded like a muffler of sound briefly dragging along the ground.

As if an eternal thing that was flying somewhere far away had stayed briefly on a certain student's lips.

A sublimely high melody that existed for only a minute.

Instead of letting out an exclamation, a student drenched with inspiration had to let out a single phrase of neutrino.

I wanted to run after it right away and pick up the world's lightest muffler of that sound,

But I held myself back awkwardly, fearful that the feeling would disappear.

And so, I couldn't even recall the song's lyrics.

A melody was neither beautiful nor sad, but an unknowable disappointment was ingrained in it.

A melody shoving itself into the regret, which comes back when one brings up the memories of the listener once again.

A melody whose beginning, end, and entirety no one could ever know.

A melody imbued with eeriness.

A melody heard not with ears but with one's whole body.

As if the net of chords was spread out carefully both outside and inside the window, and only the melody flew up from human lips.

After the song ended,

Lady No became an expression of a person who was waiting for something.

As if to capture the song, she kept her door closed for a long time.

As if to hold that ray of light that comes suddenly out from someone's dark body, passing like a single thread.

THE 'ONCE~' SIDE OF THE WORLD

Just hold on a little longer; once January comes—
Just hold on a little longer, once the boat arrives—

Once it snows.
Once we graduate.
Once the wind rises.
Once the wound heals.

We will sail on a boat and cross the ocean.

We will be carried on that boat, thinking that there will be new tidings and a new world when we arrive.

We will believe, at the very least, that we will be able to leave behind this patience, which we needed to endure on this boat.

Enduring nausea, mental breakdowns, ennui, pains, trembling, and abuses.

Our patience is suspended between '~if' and '~because'.

Sensation is an editorial organ before it is a feeling organ.
Ears erase all the sounds we heard today.
Eyes erase every single thing we saw today.
This does not mean we neither heard nor saw.
This does not mean we did not touch.
After listening, seeing, and touching, we keep around a few vague things.
Eyes, nose, lips, and ears swallowed yesterday, erasing it all.
They erased it all with something soggy like sleep. They edited.

The cargo hold of the boat is full of passengers lying down.
Crossing the endless ocean.
Enduring.

Once we arrive.

WORDS OF AN OBJECT

I think of objects and moments that serve with infinite loyalty to Lady No.

Erasers are endlessly rubbed away as they erase the words of Lady No.

Washing soaps are destroyed again and again, endlessly washing the face of Lady No.

A pot endures the water inside itself and the fire outside. And boils.

A pot that has boiled for decades lost its original color, got disfigured, and is now turning into black soot.

The chair that has received the butt of Lady No in endless repetition now makes a squeaky cracking sound of its bones cracking up every time Lady No gets up.

Among them, the most sorrowful is time, that pitiful yet effective eraser.

Time is sorrow because it is parting.

What we have parted, we cannot love again, nor can we part again.

If parting is near, it sounds like even the frying pan is crying in hollow ringing.

It sounds like the lost cell phone looking for its owner from somewhere far away.

Before its last breath, the computer is as full of sorrow as a puppy whimpering beside one's feet, so obvious with its illness that my heart sinks.

The pinnacle of this field is the robot.

The robot is now a doctor and diagnoses with electronic waves and knows how to operate, but it is never tired and never makes a mistake.

The robot speaks, "I have no emotions. But I have intelligence."

It is amazing that an object can tell us such things.

It's the first time I've seen someone say they have no emotions without any emotion.

I do not know the pain of time.

All I have are superhuman powers.

If my master desires, I can be your sparring partner, and I can also enter a robot combat tournament.

If my master is ever in danger, I will get broken in your stead.

I know that I am not alive. When it says that, it is almost terrifying.

If I were to blabber in front of the robot that I know one day I will die, what would be the use?

Even a robot knows how to say something like this.

If my master feels this is all very awkward, then you can reset me.

Then, everything that happened between us will be erased.

Once she heard this, Lady No slapped the robot.

The robot speaks,

I do not know pain.

Perhaps Lady No really wants to be someone like a robot or a robot itself.

Didn't the robot say it has no pain or feelings or longings?

Perhaps Lady No really wants to date someone like a robot or a robot itself.

They say it doesn't even have the surging red blood of a heart?

Don't they say that it will live as an eternal slave or a servant and have no feelings?

Lady No imagines reading her poems to the robot.

But they say that the robot will expand its memory storage faster than how much its master can grow, and it will eventually teach its master. They say that it will ignore its master eventually.

DISAPPEARING GENRE

Poetry is disappearing from the world.
It might as well be classified as an Intangible Cultural Heritage.

Poetry disappears and all that remains are legends of poets and rumors in the wind about poetry.
Poetry disappears and all that remains are the popular songs, traditional ballads, proverbs, prose, the truth of rumors, and similes just barely.
Poetry disappears and all that remains are books and journals of poetry.
Poetry disappears and all that remains are solipsistic essays, bellows, and modicums of behavior.
Poetry disappears and all that remains are romantic, reflectional, and pastoral songs.
Poetry disappears and all that remains are poetry education, poetry groups, and old poets.
Poetry disappears and all that remains are what poets said outside of their poems.
Poetry disappears and all that remains are rumors about the poet.
Poetry disappears and all that remains are repetitions, reproductions, repetitions again, and reproductions again.
Poetry disappears and all that remains are sentimentalism and poses.
Poetry disappears and all that remains are the uses, the functions, and the effects of poetry.
Poetry disappears and all that remains are the activations of projects for becoming a poet.

I am writing poetry.
I write within that disappearance.

COWARDLY OLD WOMAN

We were on a train from New Jersey to New York.

In front of us sat a cowardly old white woman.

You will know why she is a cowardly old woman at the end of this short episode.

Her hair was dyed yellow, but black and white roots were showing.

Her face was smothered with makeup powder

But her lips were so red that they were dark.

She kept her tri-colored hair up with a type of hairpin that had long gone out of fashion.

She was sitting on her own on a seat for three.

After the train left the station, we talked quietly while sitting behind her.

She yelled at us.

"You must be quiet in this car, stop talking, you are not the only two people in this car."

But this car wasn't one of those designated quiet cars for Washington DC commute.

Surprised by her loud yelling, other passengers looked back at us.

After some time, we whispered to each other again.

The cowardly old woman flipped her blue eyes and shushed us with her finger to her lips.

We apologized and the cowardly old woman went to sleep.

Train staff came to us. The staff person joked with us, and we laughed.

But the cowardly old woman did not shush us.

Sometime later, a group of white college students with large backpacks got on.

Making fun of someone, they laughed together.

Their voices were very loud. Their voices must have been at least forty times louder in decibel than ours.

The old woman did not say anything. She pretended to be asleep.

Was it because they spoke in English while we spoke in the language of Aerok?

Was it because they had the faces of Westerners while we had the faces of Aerok?

When Lady No stared at her while getting off the train, the old woman quickly put on her shades.

The old woman got off the train after everyone else had gotten off.

A white-haired man who was sitting across from us stood up and pointed at her, told her she was a coward.

FISH WITH SHAVEN HEADS

I spent a night at a Buddhist college for women monks.

A storm was slowly making its way up north that night.

From my sleep, I heard the symphony from the main hall, waking up the morning.

After the solitary wooden bell awakened all of creation, the temple's clear bell roused the living things of the earth, and the muted wooden clapper stirred the creatures of the water. Finally, the piercing metallic clang from the kitchen resonated with such a cry that it awakened the beings of the sky. It was a symposium of sound. After some words were spoken for the Buddha, the teachers, the parents, and the masses, a chorus chanted at the temple. When I opened the door, I saw a part of the temple opening like a lotus made from light amid the storm. The main hall was a blossom flying brightly as if it were the storm's eye.

And in the main hall, women monks with their shaven heads were chanting, bringing their small hands together like a school of fish.

When the morning came, I opened my umbrella, and I was guided by the head monk through the garden. When we crossed the paradise bridge above the valley, the monk told me a story about rain rituals the women monks used to perform.

When the night of drought comes, the women monks who were born in the year of the dragon must take a bath in the valley while wearing cauldron lids on their heads. This always brought rain. How long did they have to bathe for the rain ritual? Of course, until it rains. Like waking up all creation with their daybreak prayers, women monks once woke up the god of rain with their bathing. My umbrella flipped over, and there were fish in the strong current in the valley, and they looked like hands brought together in chorus chanting. Shaven-headed fish didn't get washed away by the rough waters. They were curled up as if they were praying.

WE HAD ALREADY USED HER UP

Now, after thirty minutes, she will arrive. Shoving chemical cotton balls into a blue-black calfskin, she has a butt risen more than thirty centimeters high. She, who can deeply bury anyone. When we place on her a cushion blooming with peonies, we will be buried in that field of flowers, or we may lie down next to the field of flowers and stretch ourselves out. We will place our feet on the weeping cello, lick the sugar jelly's skin, and wet our hands inside the sunlight thick as honey. Sweat will pour out from every pore of our bodies. It will be as if we have fallen into an ocean of jelly. We may end up falling into an anxiety that is like a peony blooming on this blue-black ocean of jelly. Eyeballs will begin to melt as if they've fallen into sweet vinegar. She will arrive soon. Strong, strapping men are bringing her on a truck. Do their forearms resemble the dark forearms of native men setting up beach chairs on a blue shoreline? Will we recite the field of peonies of brilliant sorrow there? All of our bodies melt, our nerves spreading out like soggy noodles. We are waiting for her now.

She grows old the moment she arrives. She is already outdated. While the light stays on or off in the middle of the floor, she gets old. When the fluorescent lights burn her skin, it looks as though her blue-black skin is deteriorating. When the family is out one day, I quietly look in on her, and she is completely swollen, shouldering ennui all alone, enduring the dust floating down like snow, keeping her eyes wide like they are a pair of glasses. When we look in closely with a microscope, there are ticks that look like dinosaurs reduced in size by a one-to-ten-million ratio, having made a home on her stomach, surviving by eating the dandruff off her flesh.

She is too big. There is no way to even store her somewhere. Her legs are buried and lost inside her butt. Is it because her butt is too heavy that she can't even walk on her own on the floor while everyone else is sleeping. When he returns home, he places his head on her tightly swollen left forearm and goes to sleep. Her butt slackens down whenever this happens. He caresses her butt endlessly. "It's an amazing butt," he compliments her. Sometimes he accidentally spills hot coffee on this butt. Children pierce this butt with thumbtacks. Instead of blood, dry fat spills out saying no, no.

When he sits on her, she shakes her whole body. Her body leans toward one side. Rattles. One leg gets shorter. She no longer has shame. Her underwear flows outside her skirt, and her skin blisters so much that an old cow's bones might burst out from it. No one will take her donation of organs. She must now be named defacement. Her house gets old alongside her. The pots blacken, and the grandfather clock only tells the time twice a day; a part of the ceiling slackens, as if it is holding a dead rat. All day, wearing threadbare pajamas that are as old as her bras, he does even fold his blankets.

One rainy day, someone throws her out next to a trash can. A street cat bites a piece off her stomach. Wet memories crawl out from her stomach. Memories are pungent in the rain. The man in the blanket never gets up even after she leaves their home.

WHAT DO I DO WHEN I CAN'T FORGET

We tour Confucian academies of Aerok with foreigners.

He talks about the year that the academy was founded and what its scholarship was like, even though no one asked him.

He tells us about the differences between all these academies.

Even though we tell him that all this information was available on the board outside the main gate, he keeps talking.

He will not let us experience the place ourselves.

It is impossible to imagine anyone at this academy who sat to write poems or read books.

Attempts to conjure the smell of calligraphy ink on the person grinding it—someone who, moments ago, had been deep in debate after traveling far to get here—collapse into fragments. The image of lice in their hair, their white sleeves, the dirt staining those sleeves, all shatters to smithereens under the deluge of information spilling from his words.

This time, he tells a historical tale.

Lady No imagines a sky that people, who lived under the rule of a single lord, looked up to.

She thinks about the suffocating poverty.

She thinks about the suffocating power.

She thinks about a game where, no matter how you throw, you die.

But when his story takes its turn to The Book of Changes, he starts to draw the divination diagrams on the ground, and she loses her patience and goes for a walk on her own.

His lessons continue no matter where she goes.

The foreigners don't get to experience the atmosphere of the academy and only look at his face, listening to his story.

He is about to go over the entirety of Aerok's history.

He is about to go over Chinese classics and Aerok's philosophy.

He pours out his words like someone whose storage has opened.

Wherever we go, his voice hovers about us.

When his lecturing is over, he starts to take pictures.

He wields his camera like a captor, like someone arresting the landscape.

We must assume our positions.

He seems to have an ardent faith in the famous quote that goes, 'humanity's struggle against time is the struggle of remembrance against oblivion.'

He seems to feel slight that people are oblivious to the revolutions of his youth.

He seems to devote that sense of slight to stirring up information.

When I was hiding under a wall trying to escape him, he came to me.

He asked, 'What do I need to do to write poetry?' And Lady No answered,

'How about starting by covering up what's written in your notebook?'

FATHER IS GROWING

Father is sleeping inside a dark room.
He eats breakfast and sleeps, he eats lunch and sleeps, he eats dinner and sleeps.
Lady No often forgets that her father is in there, even when she opens the door.
Father is curling beneath sheets.
Like furniture, like a bundle of blankets.

He must have spent all his fate.
After retirement, father is growing backwards.
Sometimes he is a young man, now he is a boy hanging on to his mother's skirt.
No. He is beyond gender. It is impossible to tell if he is male or female.
He keeps getting cuter and he may need a bib.
Who gave this life to father?

His hands were big, his feet were big, he was tall, my father.
My father got taller when he was on the podium.
Why did he become a bundle?
Did you tie your own earlobes up?

STAR GIVER AND STAR RECEIVER

A student came and talked.

"Teacher, one of your recent poetry books received only one star from a reader on an online bookstore."

"How many stars is a perfect score?" Lady No asked, already knowing the answer.

The student answered,

"Five stars."

The student consoled Lady No.

"You received many more stars on foreign websites for the same book, so please do not worry."

After the student left, Lady No looked up her recent book of poems on that online bookstore her student mentioned.

Indeed, one reader had given her book only one star.

Lady No thought about this.

A single star is the same thing as a minus.

Lady No swore with clenched fists that she will refuse to receive two stars from that reader and consoled herself.

(In the morning when she looked up other sites, the reader using the same nickname had given half a star to each of Lady No's books of poetry.)

Peter Handke in *The Afternoon of a Writer* realizes that he has no readers and falls into despair. He becomes fearful that "his enemies might be marching behind him when he enters an alley" during his walks, anxious that "the glowering eyes" and "the enemies of the book" are following him. Though it wasn't that bad for Lady No,

I decided that no one reads my books of poems, other than Lady No.

BEAN DISHES OF MANY COUNTRIES

Of all dishes, the ones based on beans smell like the earth of the country where the dish is from.

Japan's natto, Aerok's cheongukjang, England's baked beans, India's dal made from lentils, Mexico's chili, Portugal and Brazil's feijoada, France's cassoulet made of chickpeas, the Middle East's lentil falafel and hummus spread, all these amazingly exude the smell of their country's earth. The taste of crushed beans is so close to the taste of their earth. It's like the taste that embraces the bodies of the dead. Among them, the bean dish from Aerok has the most pungent smell.

The earth grows and flourishes life but also wants it all to die. What is born must also go away quickly so that something else can grow and flourish. The reason why Earth circles and rotates is because it is trying to 'shake off' death (apparently, somewhere in America, there is a ritual in which, when someone dies, they shake their bed so that evil spirits will be shaken off). Earth spins its wheel of time for years and centuries to make fertile soil out of us, to encourage us to be even better soil. Earth tells us to get off of here, and we try to stay here. Perhaps the hymn for life might be Earth nagging us to be brilliant soils.

Thus, every year from every corner of Earth, beans rise from soil smelling of the ancestors of that country's life.

ONE DAY I WILL CAST AWAY PERSONIFICATION

There is a level called human.
There is a level called normal human.
There is a level called modern human.
There is a level called Aerok human.

A touch of laziness on any of these rungs—neglecting to clean rooms, iron clothes, bathe, extend greetings, recognize others, step outdoors, or wave flags—and we begin falling down. Dust accumulates, clothes grow musty, and soon we're kicked off. Should one opt out of societal norms, like attending weddings or funerals, disregarding formality and institutions, the descent accelerates. From birth, we're hung up on a level. Suffering nervous breakdowns, we stand, heads held high in the void, hanging on for our dear life. Much like a temple perched on a precipice, we cling to our body's edge.

The birth of Lady No means the beginning of her personification. The education of Lady No indicates she's learning her personified role. The continued survival of Lady No suggests this fabricated virtual life has become her beacon of hope, aiding her resilience. As she persists, she approaches the moment she'll cast away her personification.

From birth, we engage in the ceaseless process of personifying ourselves. We persevere in this civilization by elevating each of our 'I,' even when the 'I' yearns to devolve into the beastliness, to succumb to death, to be deemed abnormal. We're suspended above a web of language.

Now is when Lady No scribbles a few words amidst lines she is writing. Now is when she consistently casts the persona known as Lady No atop the moment called now, now, now. This is resilience stretched to its limit.

Lady No is certain she'll transcend this personification someday.

And more than that, she senses an ineffable surge beyond words, awaiting her.

Bare-naked, she anticipates confronting something beyond human origin.

Perhaps Lady No yearns for that sight—the vast, lucid visage oscillating across the cosmos, that defining moment when self is rendered redundant.

Though Lady No writes poetry to shun personification, she ironically employs rhetoric in the process. To carry Lady No far away to a place beyond the reach of personification. To unchain the chain that has become the mind of Lady No. To a realm where one sheds all pretense and merely exists. To that moment of shining formlessness. To bring Lady No there from time to time. To jump off from the levels of human, normal human, modern human, and Aerok human.

To be oneself in one's own universe.
To be a soul.

CHOICE

(There is a building at the symbolic center of Aerok. What happened happened in a corner room of this building.)

A meeting for the selection of a poetry award winner was being held there.
This was the third meeting, and we were to pick the winner that day.
There are many criteria that can be used to categorize the five judges.

Gender: 4 males, 1 female.
Genre: 3 poets, 1 critic.
Aerok-style criteria: 2 realists, 2 modernists, 1 ambiguous (the criteria for these categories is automatically applied to anyone who is over the age of fifty, but not so for anyone below fifty, or sometimes it is not even considered).
Worldview: Aesthetic Rationality, Traditional Lyricism, Everyday Editor, Womanhood, Modernism (these are categories used by journalists).
Job: 1 retired professor, 3 active professors, 1 editor at a publishing house.
Majors: 2 Aerok literature–related majors, 3 foreign literature–related majors.
Hair: 4 black hairs, 1 white hair (People of Aerok are born with black hair, so it does not work as a category for them. This is the same for eye colors. There are only various shades from brown to black. So we do not categorize human beings according to the colors of their eyes. In ancient texts they said that women with darker eyes are more beautiful, but now women of Aerok sometimes wear colored contact lenses because they do not like their dark eyes).

Political alignments: 1 man categorized as leftist, 1 man categorized as right wing, 3 men and women who have never been categorized as either.

Marital status: all 5 are married (marital status is also not important. 90 percent of people above age 50 in Aerok are married, no question).

Incarceration status: 1 person who went to prison, 3 people who may or may not have gone to jail, 1 person has never been to jail (prison experience is important. If he has been to prison, then it is proof that he is a practitioner of Realist literature who lived through the dictatorships of the 1970s–80s. It tells us that he prefers the opposition party that is not in power, and that he is a leftist. The fact of his incarceration is an important barometer proving to us that his poetry is in transition from poems about resistance to poems about love, traveling, regression, glorification of motherhood, infatuation with Buddhism, et cetera).

Shoes: 3 black, 2 brown.
Jacket: 1 checkered pattern, 1 black, 1 grey, 1 brown.
Drink: 2 coffees, 2 green teas, 1 water.
Glasses: 3 wearing, 2 non-wearing.
Reading glasses during the selection process: 5 wearing.
Residential locations in Seoul: 4 Gangbuk, 1 Gangnam.

(According to journalists, the books of poetry can be categorized by using the following criteria.)

Traditional lyric
Rural
Resistance
Philosophy
Abstraction
Ambiguous (not even the journalists have tried to categorize them)
Travel
Popular

Living things + natural law + veteran
Rhetoric

(The five judges had met twice in the previous month and had narrowed down the list of ten books to four. The remaining four books were as follows.)

Traditional lyric
Rural
Philosophy
Resistance

(One of them had to be chosen that day as the winner.)

Opinions were shared.
Lady No talked and wrote things down.

About "Traditional lyric"
It has received too many awards recently.
It is not as good as it used to be.
It is copying the entertainment of the gentlemen-scholars of the Chosun Dynasty.
It is copying the attitudes of carefree lifestyles of literary men of the past.
It loves wandering and drinking and women without any interiority nor social criticism nor incisive commentary nor wit.
It loves its blank spaces.
It writes like Du Fu.
It is kind of disappointing.

About "Rural"
It acts like a child.
It cannot be translated into a foreign language.

It is a beautiful painting of a landscape.

It is a child-like slice-of-life of an adult farmer.

How can someone who works as a professor write these naïve scenes of farm laborers.

It is the epitome of purity.

It is purity that is camouflaged with barriers.

About "Philosophy"

What does this even say.

I have been reading poetry for decades. But I don't know. If I don't know who can know?

Let's say this is translated. Who will understand this.

Who were the preliminary judges. Their tastes are questionable.

It is good that there are parts we can say we don't know.

It is philosophy of the every day. It is philosophy of the quotidian. It is the omission of the mundane specificity.

It is perhaps the extrication of the external, the extraction of it.

It is a deep interrogation of time and being.

It is a link in the chain of the struggle to blow out the self.

It is similar to the work of Octavio Paz.

It is highly recommended.

Give an interpretation of this work if you can.

An interpretation is given using one of the poems as an example.

Isn't that interpretation more like poetry that the work it purports to interpret.

About "Resistance"

Revolution was given up and the poet went to stay at temples instead. Disappointing.

The work reflects on one's own failures while also having the power to strike directly with a message.

Where is revolution and resistance, where are the reflections and remorse.

This isn't prosaic, this is just prose.

It does not point toward the externality of life within the interiority of life, it only despairs about the externality that always exists. That is why it is prose.

It came out from the actual prison and now struggles within the prison of time. Buddhism, dance, meditating to be a bodhisattva, these are all escapisms. Why do all the failed revolutionaries of Aerok go away to temples. They don't just go to temples. They go to women, too.

Isn't the path of such a life beautiful.

Doesn't it feel, after reading this, like you just saw Marx fornicating with a servant girl.

5 laughs
42 silences

Discussion didn't lead to any agreement, so we decided to vote by narrowing the list down to a final two.

We each wrote the names of two people on scraps of paper. So that we could keep a record of them.

2 votes for Traditional Lyric, 2 votes for Philosophy, 3 votes for Rural, 3 votes for Resistance.

We decided to discuss only "Rural" and "Resistance," each of which got 3 votes, but it took a long time.

During this process one of the judges gave up their vote, shouting, "I don't like this kind of democracy!" and proclaimed that they wouldn't participate in the next vote. They argued in favor of "Philosophy" until the end.

And so, "Resistance" received 3 votes in the final round and was selected as the winner. The poet, who was also an editor, the one who argued for "Rural" until the end, left without saying goodbye.

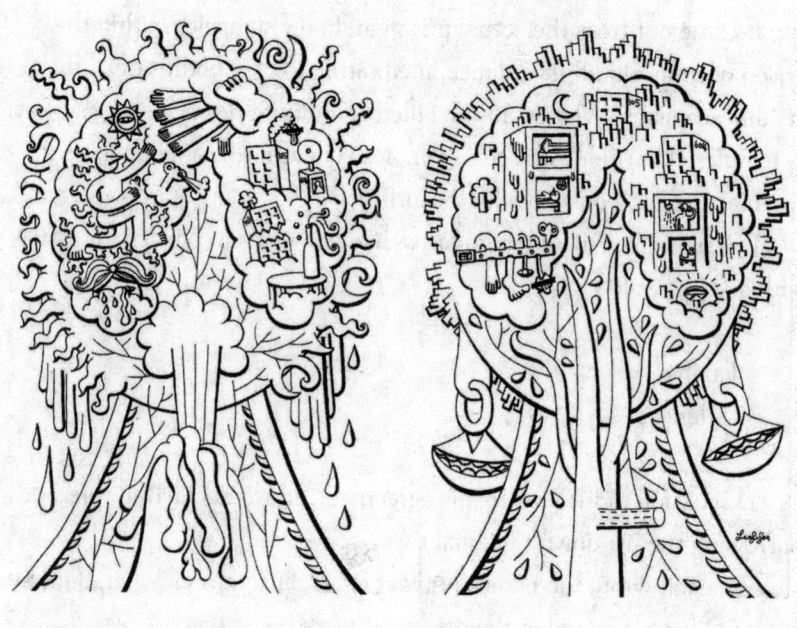

PHONE CALL

A phone call from her dead maternal grandmother.
Lady No doesn't answer. But a voice is recorded.
"Come out, I am waiting, I am in front of the subway station's exit No. 1."

A phone call from her dead maternal grandmother.
Lady No doesn't answer. But a voice is recorded.
"Come out, I am still waiting, I am in front of the subway station exit No. 1."
And it keeps getting recorded.

Out of options, Lady No decides to go out.
She changes her clothes, looks for her shoes.
But none of the shoes fit her.
She goes out, dragging her big slippers.
While on her way, her slippers come off.

Grandmother is waiting for her, but her feet won't move forward.
She sees her grandmother standing in front of the subway station's exit No. 1.
The poor thing.
She seems cold.
I want to give her all of Lady No until nothing is left.
But the shoes keep coming off.

My family tells me in the morning.
"If Lady No had reached station exit No. 1, then Lady No would not be having her breakfast with her family."
That is how it is. The living cannot reach the dead even in dreams.

PRINCESSES IN FORMALDEHYDE

To be in this world, their heads bowed at a slant, sweating profusely, dressed in pink.

At the bottom of this world, someone is getting slapped, without anyone knowing, bound in the basement, dressed in pink. Conceding victory to a man who has lost his mind, their disappearance is nearing.

Why do they hate women, binding them, hitting them, stealing their money?
Stealing women, making women disappear, making women shudder, finding their self-respect through women.

Are pupils made of water?
The day the river lights up a thousand, ten thousand pupils.

Women are imprisoned inside basements, mountains, living rooms, and oceans, as if they are floating in formaldehyde.

Before the fairy tales became processed and manufactured, didn't their original versions show that the princesses were already in rigor mortis? Wasn't it the case that the sleeping princesses were not waiting for their princes? Wasn't it the case that it was the princes who murdered them?

Whenever we share the stories of disappeared women, the remaining women shudder in fear.

A friend of Lady No created a memorial website for women who lost their lives to violence,

A site that prayed for the peaceful rest of disappeared women.

A site that made you press your palms together in prayer upon seeing its first page.

But, like women drowned in formaldehyde, the site was submerged in the liquid of sneers. Eventually, it had to shut down.

ARE YOU A MEMBER?

I go to Mom's house.
Mom informs me that some long-time writer in that province is coming to meet Lady No.
He brings dried persimmons.
He asks Lady No.
Are you a member of PEN?
No.
Are you a member of Writers' Association?
No.
Do you have a poem of yours displayed in the subway stations of Seoul?
No.
Is there a monument for your poems erected somewhere?
No.
He is sorely disappointed.
He no longer wants to speak to Lady No.
But Lady No tells him to have tea.
He drinks tea for a bit and leaves.
He is greatly disappointed by the daughter of a mother.
He leaves behind dried persimmons.

AUDACIOUS RESOLVE

Lady No decides to put a cuss in all her poems from now on.

Lady No will put a cuss in at the end of all the documents she submits to her superior from now on.

It will be like that rumor about a singer whose songs cursed you when you played them backward.

Lady No will let out a good, sharp cuss first in the morning to start her day from now on.

Cussing about Lady No who hasn't yet learned how to let go completely.

Cussing about Lady No who has fallen into despair and can't bring herself to bury her work.

Cussing about Lady No who is writing letters of apology like a child in the remaining study period.

Cussing about her pathetic belief that nothingness has not yet arrived while going down the staircase every day to be shipwrecked.

Cussing about her empty faith that Lady No's writings are translations of the others and the world who have come crashing into her.

Cussing about her sorrowful remembrance that the poetry Lady No has constructed has destroyed Lady No, turning her into something that Lady No isn't.

In I intend to return the diagnosis of neurological anxiety, autonomic imbalance, low blood pressure, 3rd neuralgia, vestibular organ disorder, headaches, dizziness, etc., etc.

SEPTEMBER

DMZ GREEN

For the first time in her life, Lady No traveled to the northernmost point accessible from southern Aerok.

It was a place where language spontaneously emerged wherever a work of art was placed. This phenomenon appeared to arise from the hidden narratives embedded in the landscape conversing with the artworks. The language of ghosts was swarming in the air.

Surveying the area from the observatory, all was green.

The green, like rust clutching an old padlock, had gripped the memory of war tightly for decades.

Once, after ascending to the summit of a mountain exceeding five thousand meters and descending to the timberline, it appeared as though the green was clinging stubbornly to the life force of Earth, refusing to release its hold. The terror of the green was palpable then, and now the same fear arose for the green grasping the waist of Aerok.

Southern and northern soldiers stood watch over the green's terror.

They were guardians of the silent green.

The green, ready to explode at a touch.

The green, primed to detonate beneath a footfall.

The green whose shattering silence will kill us all.

The terror of the green.

IS REUNIFICATION POSSIBLE WITHOUT WAR?

Jessie Jones lives in Dublin.
Her brother is a medium.
Her performance, titled Another Drum, was held
At the Iron Triangle War Memorial Tourist Center
And it was also performed in Northern Ireland.
Jessie Jones begins her performance by handing out cards to her audience.
Then, they are asked to prepare one heartfelt question each.
Then, the tarot specialist divines every answer according to each question.

She received five questions first.
"Will we be reunified in ten years?"
"Will the great powers want our reunification?"
"Do North and South want reunification?"
"Is it feasible for the Sunshine Policy to continue?"
And a question from a child, "Is reunification possible without a war?," received the biggest applause.
Jessie answered each question.
The divination of cards is dependent on the interpreter, yet there were many positive answers.

I thought about 'a work that proceeds according to the method of heartfelt questions.'
I thought about 'a trip that proceeds according to the method of heartfelt questions.'

Partings, turbulences, conservatives and progressives, corrupt politics, crisis, refugee consciousness, hatred, pride, impatience, powerlessness, etc., etc.

I thought about the shadows of the division that hide deep within the bodies of all the people of Aerok.

I thought about the stories DMZ green keeps locked up.

'Will we get a chance to have a picnic on the meadow, underneath a streetlamp at the DMZ park?' Lady No wrote on her card.

RECIPES DURING BOMBARDMENT

My teacher hid in the attic of his brother's house.

It was during the war, and they were fearful he would be captured by soldiers.

He ate food that his sister-in-law snuck in.

I dared not ask how he dealt with his bowel movements.

For he was a solemn teacher.

My teacher said that he read his sister-in-law's Japanese version of "The Encyclopedia of World Cuisine" in that attic.

He read it so many times that he now knows almost all the major recipes from around the world.

After he read the cookbook, he said that he imagined dishes that mixed all the different countries' food, a kind of fusion dish.

My teacher said that in the attic he lived in the imagined world of tastes.

He now knows how to make all the dishes from around the world with his language.

That is why when my teacher goes to a restaurant, he always talks to the chef.

Even about all the different sauces that we don't know about.

However, because his wife banned him from the kitchen, he said that he never gets to cook. Today when we went to a restaurant, the chef there got so excited because my teacher knew about a dish that no one makes anymore. Of course, my teacher was the master of dishes that he had never eaten before.

ENTRANCE EXAM

The day the applicants came to take the exam, it snowed.
Lady No slowly walked the hallways.

A thousand students were writing poems that had to be titled 'morning alley.'
A thousand were thinking of 'morning alley' at the same time.

'Morning alley' also brightened inside Lady No's head.
Snow fell, and in a place that was not real, that was also not death, a 'morning alley' opened.
Lady No looked back and forth at the applicants in the classrooms and the snow outside the window. It felt like watching an angel standing in the snowy landscape. Lady No saw a picture of a 'morning alley' that had suddenly appeared inside her head.

In that picture, I thought about the thousand souls, who were trying to turn on even fainter images. I thought about the sensitivity of the applicants, absent yet floating, writing poems as they held up their faint images and walked into their own pictures.
There were 'morning alleys' everywhere. There were a thousand of them. There was a 'morning alley' even if its streetlamp was on or off.

After a little while, Lady No felt like she had been to a thousand 'morning alleys',
To these alleys without anyone there, to these alleys with cold faces that seemed to be wanting for nothing other than Lady No's disappearance.

But soon, the morning of harsh discrimination will arrive, and some will be accepted, others rejected.

And just before that, there was 'morning alley', small barely coming to light, in its silence. And before that arrival, 'morning alley' was small, barely coming to light, in its silence.

TEACHER BUYS ME A MEAL

"There is a pain in your poetry these days, let me buy you a meal."
Lady No visited her teacher to get her meal.
After their meal, the teacher talked to her.
"Stop writing poems like that, so difficult!
Please stop writing difficult poetry, I get angry when I read it!
Write poems that a toddler can understand, don't talk about bad things in poems!
I've wanted to tell you this since your debut, but I am saying it now!
Isn't poetry supposed to give solace and vision? Not sterility!
Seek facts and truths!"
While listening to this, a funeral hearse of purest white passed by Lady No.
Compared to funeral hearses that Lady No saw in her childhood, which were flamboyant with flowers, this white hearse was strange.
Lady No tore apart her books of poetry to fold beautiful flowers. The book was so big that it was hard to flip through it and it was difficult to tear out the pages, but they were still foldable.
White flowers filled her room. Lady No built one hearse of white flowers with one book of poetry and floated it on the water. After a hearse floated away, another hearse left. "When did I write so many poems?" She kept making hearses.
Folding papers and then cutting them swiftly with scissors, like women shamans with swords about to perform the ritual for placating the dead, she crafted one white flower after another. She made Taean Seolwi-Seolgyeong. The sunlight that came through the window roasted Lady No's hands whitest white.

When I opened my eyes and looked at my teacher, my teacher was wiping the ketchup from his mouth saying let's go.

Lady No mumbled that she didn't know what the teacher meant by easy-to-read poetry.

She saw hundreds of white funeral hearses parked in the parking lot beyond the window.

Teacher, goodbye.

Teacher, doesn't poetry pursue the impossibility of what is believed to exist? The truth, the real—don't such things turn out to be nonexistent once you actually pursue them? Isn't the pursuit itself poetry?

Lady No mumbled to herself and went to get on a hearse.

Looking for another difficult poem.

VIRGINHOOD AND MOTHERHOOD

Finally, the dreams of taking exams have disappeared.
What a relief, but then a dream began where a rough man kept chasing me.
A dream where a worker with a pickaxe came looking for me.
A dream where an old teacher, who kept trying to sexually harass me, chased after me.

A dream where a man, who tenaciously kept postponing our breakup, chased me on horseback.

When I woke up from those dreams, the world was awash in broad daylight and the peace of the morning was so sweet.

But after a while, a dream where I lost my child came for me.
In that dream, phone buttons refused to be pushed.
Police always ignored the woman's words.

The child disappeared somewhere no one knows.
A mother running barefoot to find the child who disappeared into the desolate riverbank.

And then, I push my ear against the room where the child is sleeping.
What a relief. The child is breathing.
The child is still behind the closed door, and
The rough world is outside the door.

Women keep dreaming two dreams back and forth.

One in which virginhood is lost and the other in which motherhood is lost.

Virginhood is the transparent peculiarity one has kept since birth.

It does not disappear after the first time in bed.

It is the transparent center that women keep forever.

It cannot be dirtied, nor can it be shattered.

It is the overwhelming frailty that women forever keep. It is a secret.

Colette said that maternal love is banal.

Once we are liberated from sexual and maternal love, she said,

We will experience everything in the world with joy in all the multiplicities,

But women are always bound to motherhood.

It does not disappear because we choose not to have children.

It is the peace of transition of a body as a gift, a body that embraces another.

It is the overwhelming part of the frailty women hold, the future of it, the pity of it, the thing we can throw away.

NORTH MOUNTAIN

North Mountain likes me, thought Lady No.
She sang songs to North Mountain
And caressed its changing face and arms through spring, summer, fall, and winter.
A great and sensitive sorrow was ingrained in North Mountain, which a finite being couldn't begin to comprehend.

She played with the magpies that lived on North Mountain, and she smiled at the face of North Mountain when it rained.
She liked it so much that she prayed, O North Mountain, may you last eternal!

Today, while walking on North Mountain, I thought about Tibet's sky burial undertakers.
The story of how they fold a dead person up and wrap them up in blankets
And carry them away on carts or carry them on their backs.
Immediate family cannot follow them, only their distant relatives.
And then, the fabric merchant goes into a small house in the mountain
And takes off the clothes of the dead and throws them out
And cuts up the body into pieces, men or women or old or young,
And gives the pieces to eagles.

The sight of a sky burial undertaker calling for eagles while holding up pieces of human flesh.
A monk dressed in red drapes playing a pipe made of oily thigh bones.

Lady No stayed with these thoughts as if she smelled the smell of that high mountain, a cutting board for corpses.

The moment when Lady No's thoughts were about to call forth eagles.

North Mountain threw Lady No out and snapped her arms.

Lady No swallowed her screams six times like a crow in the heart of North Mountain.

Until now, Lady No had thought that North Mountain liked her.

I think about North Mountain even at the ER.
My eyes fill with tears because it feels like North Mountain pushed Lady No out.

Tears come because it feels like I've said something blasphemous through my lips.

Tears come again because I feel like I've been cast out by North Mountain.

RODRIGUEZ AND RODRIGUEZ

Cape Town Sugaman and Detroit Sugaman.

Cape Town Sugaman sings.
Detroit Sugaman labors.

Cape Town Sugaman explodes in infinite sequence.
His song floats high above Cape Town.
Detroit Sugaman labors in infinite sequence.
He deconstructs a house and builds another. A day laborer.

Cape Town Sugaman is incubating.
Detroit Sugaman is growing old.

Cape Town Sugaman lives in poignant mythology.
Detroit Sugaman lives in daily society.

Song comes alive in Cape Town and mixes its body with revolution.
Song is dead in Detroit. Song is in the grave.
Rodriguez and Rodriguez walk while carrying bags.
When they walk in symmetry to the equator and the meridian,
they are two people and one person at the same time.

Detroit Sugaman says to Cape Town Sugaman,
"You are my image that I drew."

Half is a song. The other half is labor.
Half is a guitar case. The other half is a tool bag.

Two men walk through absolute silence.

A mirror placed in between. One side is Africa, the other is America.

When you look at the mirror from South Africa, you see North America. When you look at the mirror from North America, you see South Africa.

When the sun sets here,
The sun rises over there.
We don't have a soul here.
They don't have a body there.

As if a dead singer's soul suddenly rose out of his grave.
As if the soul of song went around Earth.

Here is a street corner that takes you there.
There is a street corner that takes you here.

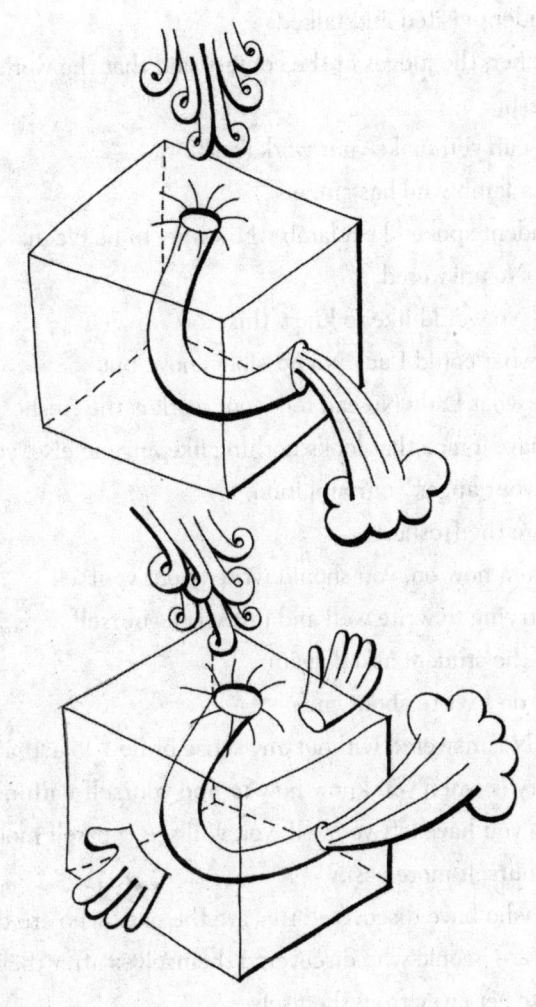

LIKE FRESH FOOD

A student visited and talked.

"Teacher, the judges of the contest said that the work I submitted wasn't fresh.

How can you make your work fresh?"

Like a lamb who has sinned,

A student spoke like a lamb who wants to be clean.

Lady No answered.

Lady No would like to know this, too,

And what could Lady No possibly know, but

From what Lady No can tell, your work is the freshest!

You have a face that looks nothing like anyone else, your inferiority complex, your anger, your ambition,

You are the freshest.

So, from now on, you should write about yourself.

Stop trying to write well and just write yourself.

Then the student asked again.

"How do I write about 'me'?"

Lady No answered without any sense of how to actually do that.

"Poetry is when you know how to find yourself within yourself.

When you have left yourself, you will see yourself more clearly and discover yourself more easily.

Ones who have discovered this are the ones who are called poets.

Poets are people who discovered themselves after they themselves managed to get away from themselves."

SILENCE PRODUCING MACHINES

—Hemingway once said that the writer's work is to get silence dressed. Put a pair of pants on silence, put a jacket on silence, make it go to the sea, make it row on a boat, or make it go out on a battlefield. Make silence get dressed and get drunk on battlefields, make it fight, make it live in debauchery, and pass through the first world war, the second world war, and the third world war. A work of listening to the silence of silence again.

—After communication disappears between two people, silence is produced. The silence between Freud and Jung after they went their separate ways. The silence that boils between people who broke up. The screaming of that silence.

—The work of listening closely to the words of the people who disappeared into silence, or the work of calmly accepting the words of silence that are like erasers and erasing myself, or the work of dressing the noise with clothes of silence. The work of poets.

—Today silence does not exist anywhere in the world. The silence can only be recorded by putting a mic into a vacuum-sealed box. That is what the sound director said.

—But where do we look for specimens of painful silence? Where do we record their soundless screams? Where are the ears that will hear their first words?

—Perhaps they drowned in the silence that attacks the people who have fallen into silence. Perhaps we are fooling ourselves thinking that it will work out if we can put a mic into the nucleus of that silence. Only if we could hear its voice. Only if that was possible. Time that is not time. Silence that has congealed tenderly like tofu or jelly surrounds us. It is a silence that won't be split until 'I' bring a knife. Let us shatter this powerless silence and listen to the pitiful silence hidden deep within.

LAUDATION

The teacher's students held a thesis dedication ceremony.
Students who wrote their thesis under his advising came to see him.
The flower petals fell slowly on a bright spring day.
We saw the teacher's six photographs.
We saw him in his teens, twenties, thirties, forties, fifties, and sixties.
The process through which he slowly grew up and neared his retirement.
But the most memorable thing was when all the old students rose
And sang full-throated the song "Teacher's Grace."
The teacher sat demurely while everyone else stood up and made sound with their mouths.
Our voices spread into the sunshine of a spring day outside the window.
But perhaps the most precious moment was the laudation given by the final student assistant of the teacher.
The assistant said that the teacher used to hold a book in one hand and a fan in the other, wrestling through the day
Until he said "Hey!" which meant it was time for dinner.
It was time for them to go out into the night's streets together.
And after the teacher left, 'hey' sat on the teacher's chair.
The teacher's place was only that chair.
The place where a major novel of Aerok's literary history was written.
Once, in its place, there used to be a broken chair that leaned a little.

WE NEED MARTYRDOM IN MODERN TOO

It could be said nowadays that the old divisions are no longer tenable, and Lady No believes that such division has always been impossible, but it is true that there have always been two political camps in Aerok's literature. In past generations of Aerok, literary folks practicing Realism possessed clarity of vision in their politics, which often led to their martyrdom, going in and out of prisons.

On the other hand, accusations have been thrown at those who get categorized as practitioners of Modernism, and they are told that their works are created solely for the sake of craft, that such works are not literature. Much advice has been given to them that they should come out and swim into the ocean of politics, into the ocean of society.

But even after hearing all such advice, they continue practicing Modernism, drawing lines, making graphs, piling up bricks, designing seemingly useless structures, talking nonsense like ghosts shelling millet, accepting constant criticism, which can't be possible if they didn't have faith in what they do. They discovered that they have a layer of senses that are not like the others, and they know how to see the imagined world and the real world as equals. They construct the worlds of language, pushing for such worlds to be realized. How can they do any of that without having the madness of martyrs?

How can we call any writing a work of literature when it doesn't ultimately surge into meaninglessness? The magic of words connecting in the resonance of their own interiorities, the ability to visualize the faith in catching the light of an image, such things are impossible without having the attitude of martyrs.

Draping oneself with total misunderstanding, as if it were a great mansion, and enduring every moment in this refusal to yield.

Believing that well-made absence is literature. Constructing the irrationality of illusions, which senses can't even recognize, again as an irrationality. Placing the two men underneath a tree as they wait for Godot. Becoming the first possessor of the future of absence, only to burn one's own work in the end.

Called out for being an irresponsible lumpen. Attacked for being a mere human without determination who dares to construct worlds made only of language. Ending up with pathological symptoms. And then, somehow, bringing and holding out yet another world once again.

Lady No thinks that some martyrdoms are like the creation of sand mandalas, those beautiful patterns that the Tibetan monks make. The precious sand patterns that will not be exchanged for the entire world, the martyrdom of a pattern that is blown out once it is finished.

An act that dreams of life even in a dream.

WE PROTECT STRANGERS' SLEEP

A voice of a stranger, or perhaps military boots and fists, can pierce through heavy sleep.

On the opposite end of things, there are gestures, and feelings, that won't dare wake us from our sleeps of exhaustion.
I heard a story about a mother who called an ambulance because of her stomach swelling,
And she refused to wake up her son from his exhausted sleep.
This made me think about the people who couldn't, or didn't, wake Lady No from her sleep.

There was a phone call from my mother.
"Your father passed away at 4 in the morning."
"Why are you calling me only now?"
"I wanted to let you know when you woke up."
My mother had been looking at his corpse for three hours alone.
"But Mom, where are you now?"
"Beside your father."
"Where is my father?"
"I said he is gone."

Darkness took me while I was holding my receiver.

A phone call came for the family sleeping in the adjacent room.
"Have breakfast on your own."
"Where are you?"
"In my room."
"What are you doing?"

"I hurt my leg last night, I called a taxi with a wheelchair service."
"Why didn't you wake me up?"
"Because the taxi was going to come in the morning anyway."
"How bad is it?"
"Bearable."

Darkness took me while I was holding my receiver.

I I I I

Stuck on the window,
Does the cicada cry I I I I.
Sticking its lips into the manger,
Does the pig cry I I I I.
I am hungry. I want to die. I want to see.
Does Lady No also cry I I I I.
Do all the I's cry I all throughout I's life.
I, the name I will die calling!

Does the water drip from the faucet like I I I I.
Does the smoke from the mister's cigarette rise like I I I I.

Dressed in a soul wearing necklaces and earrings,
Do all the I's cry I I I I.

I whom I have been and always will be!
I whom I have been and already is!
O the days when I could never be I.

Why do I put I at the front of every sentence?

Why am I nothing when I fall away from I?

Why do I call I I I I
And not know that I am becoming distant from I?

I have given birth to so many. Every day I have given birth to I's I's I's I

But how could I not have given birth to all the I's yet!

Beneath my feet, lukewarm plastic bags that I took off are piling up.

Am I a spring that gives birth to I? A mirage?
Am I a fountain that can only exist when I surge with I?

BOOKSTORE OF MY MATERNAL GRANDFATHER

Lady No was born in her maternal grandfather's bookstore.

The smell of old books and old people intermingled in that house.

The second floor was an inventory filled with books.

I pulled out books from the shelves there and sat in the green velvet swivel chair.

I looked at the books of grown-ups.

When I read these books on the floor that I sometimes couldn't understand,

Lady No often rolled to the corner of the room because the second floor was leaning a little.

The rusted tin bookstore sign outside the window was so close I thought I could touch it.

After finishing a book, I hugged it tightly.

I was still looking at a book when my grandfather was taken to a hospital.

I wept as I was looking at a book.

I was still reading a book when my grandfather's body arrived.

I could hear people calling for Lady No, but I didn't go downstairs.

My mother gave birth to my younger sibling, but her breast milk had dried up, so she dried and kept white rice cakes on the second floor.

Lady No took a few of those cakes, packed a few books, and left home.

And for a week, she was a runaway with her grandfather.

Now the books are gone, and Lady No is gone, and that house is gone, too.

The words of the books are gone, too.

A few days ago, I passed beneath my grandfather's grave when I was traveling with my friends.

Lady No said, "Hello, Grandpa."

"My house isn't a bookstore, but books fill up my room like it is an inventory."

That is how I greeted him.

WALKING IN NEW YORK

This is how you go for a walk in New Babylon.
Passing by "I'm sorry!"
Passing by "It's okay!"
Passing by "Excuse me."
Passing by "Of course!"
Passing by "You got change?"
Passing by "Thank you!"
Passing by "Can you take our photo?"
Passing by "Have a nice day!"
Passing by "Take care of yourself!"

It's a place where even babies may need to put on diapers while walking.
It's a place where one may need to eat noodles while walking.

As if people have bombs in their bags that will explode if they stop. Keep going! Persevere!

People who can say anything
But can no longer say anything.

Mumbling the same words probably bought from vending machines,
They must walk fast.

If they stop walking, it is as if the solar-powered radios
Will whisper to them three hundred ways to die.

At night, like wet underwear, eyelids descend.

YETI

It rained for days and nights. I was looking for the yeti in the murals and mandala paintings of the temple. A woman of white hair dressed in a white dress fluttered in the wind. A woman with wet eyes. A woman whose wet eyes burned with grief. Long white hair covering the yeti's face tossed and turned like the white leaves of a willow tree. A woman who left behind big footprints, no camera lens ever capturing her. A woman who spoke like the wind. A woman who ground her teeth like the wind. A woman who laughed like the wind. A woman who whispered like the wind. A woman who wept a long time because she couldn't talk—couldn't talk like the wind. While we slept in a dirty mud hut under the temple, my bed floated into the air. Someone shook Lady No out of her sleep. "Look at the yeti. She is right outside." When I opened the window, there was a snow person as white as white can be. A woman of white in grand dishevelment. A woman unseen, covered underneath her white hair that grew all over her body. A fluttering woman. When I woke up, I wanted to tell my companions that the yeti came to visit last night, but suddenly my voice wouldn't come out. I had become mute. I thought the dream had given the woman to Lady No. In the dream was a dream, and yet another dream that was deeper still. A woman of wind, who seemed to have come from that deepmost place, came and went as white as white can be, like a soul that came from the body of a snowy mountain far away.

TO FEED AND KEEP
ALIVE THE RHYTHM

Poetry is a poet's thrashing to take off the rhythm that lives on her like a parasite.

It is not a method of existence but of deficiency.

A poet is someone who has no choice but to feed and keep alive that eternally bare-naked music with neither meaning nor message.

It is the poet's other self, but the poet does not know that it is her other self.

It is always clearing its throat. It is always taking off the poet's clothes.

(But if it isn't around, then the poet can't even begin her poem.)

It came from the poet's body, but it is the poet's other self that acts like it grew up in an orphanage.

The heart-throbbing that comes reluctantly.

It is what makes one start again after constant hesitation.

It is not moral. It is not a melody.

It is not a metaphor but a world of presence.

It is not history but a world of repetition.

(Then what the hell is it?)

It is what brings fear.

It dances like fire. It moves with its own will.

It is sporadic before it is majestic.

It is what eternally returns.

It is the storage of gestures.

It is transparent.

It is what begins again and again.

But it is the majesty between lives.

It began from an orphanage, but it is not an orphan. It belongs to the one who honors it.

It is the movement going in the opposite direction of gravity.

It is the lightness of every ounce of one's strength. It is breathing (when does breathing begin for a fetus?).

But it is a deficiency that can't be cast out.

It is a deficiency that has become an instrument.

It is the first rolling of a raft that one got on before beginning the adventure into the infinite.

The infinity is merely a variation of the rolling and sloshing while sailing on this thing.

It is a wave made out of a mirror.

And waves bring pattern, and pattern brings rhythm, and the end!

But even the poet doesn't know where it will reach.

Poetry is what feeds the shameless waves.

Thus, poetry disappears into the rhythm.

HOLIDAYS

Parents were leaning a little closer to death,
And nephews had grown taller.
Everyone in our family was leaning closer to death.
We celebrated this.

We opened arms to welcome
The holiday that, like a honeybee,
Approached to nibble away at family time
While feeding on sweet things.
We let them have our bodies.

We are getting one step closer to the time
When all the animals will be extinct and only humanity will remain.
Earth where only humanity will be storing protein.

LET ME HEAL YOU

Sometimes the inevitable comes crashing down.

Sometimes the thing that was avoided again and again comes crashing down.

Because it came from eternity, we have no choice but to accept it.

Whether it comes like a storm or a gentle shower, there is a thing that we can't stop with our hands.

There is something that is always a defeat.

There is something connected to an unknowable essence that all one can do is circle around it.

Something that makes us despair forever.

There is something that perishes us when we are before it. 'I' dies there.

That is what tragedy is.

But has there been a tragedy in the history of Aerok's literature?

Was there a protagonist, who was destroyed after confronting eternal despair, in our classics?

We don't have the Devil, but we have dokkaebi.

And our heroes were saved with the help of those being. Their problems were resolved, healed, and ended in happy harmony.

In our classics and myths, much happened, but there were no tragedies.

Lady No thought that this was because we haven't pursued everything to its end.

There are people who write letters and send emails to Lady No asking for permission to use her poems to heal people's minds. They say they will heal the others even though no one asked. There are people who would console other people. Even if one says please leave me alone, they demand that you be healed, since I have an amazing method, accept my guidance. So, let's get you stitched quick.

The tragedy is hidden behind the healing dramas and the moving stories and the heart-silencing sentimentalism.

SCARY COMMUNITY

Lady No gets scared when she sees how matchsticks are gathered perfectly inside a matchbox.

Matchsticks look like soldiers wearing pink steel helmets.

Lady No is so scared she can't even open a matchbox.

The matches that already turned into fire have all left, but the heads of matches that aren't yet fire are stuck inside each box, overcrowding each place.

Toothpicks are scary, too. Are they not in perfect agreement with one another, standing in such tight formation inside such tiny tubes, waiting to get out so that they can pick away at someone else's teeth?

Sesame peppered breads are scary, too. Sesame heads are so scary.

Black sesame seeds are especially scary.

The truck with a full load of industrial pipes driving in front of me is scary. It is scary to chase after those pipes that all have uniformly sized holes.

Whose holes are they trying to be, all going together like a mob?

Hedgehog's needles in perfect formation are scary. Boots of soldiers in marching formations are scary.

People flooding into the subway's transfer stations are scary. People who hit the bottom are still at the bottom, and those who can kick themselves off from the bottom with their feet can leave the bottom.

Honeybees filling up their beehives are scary.

Tiny lifeforms constantly looking for ways to push into our holes are scary.

When one roughs it in the wilds of a tundra, bugs flood into every orifice of one's body.

When one walks into a desert storm, the sands build a house inside every orifice of one's body. One's bed gets filled with sands even after many days and nights of dusting and washing.

Pink babies of field mice, filling up all the unseen holes underneath a field, are scary.

Lady No must have some kind of obsession or phobia about anything that grows in crowds. She must have a swarm-phobia.

Is it because she lived in a house with many siblings? Is it a refugee mindset that has been branded on her genes?

When we stop breathing, I am scared of the microscopic organisms that run to us, declaring that they are the masters of our bodies.

Unity, duty, communal fate, and assemblages are all scary.

Lady No is scared of the community of destiny.

She is scared of movies that sell ten million tickets in a country of fifty million.

She is scared of people who cry all at the same time at the same scene of such movies.

She is scared of public spaces that are filled with dangers that can kill everyone at once.

She is scared of buses full of children.

RATTLE

I crossed the sea to reach China.

The big boat shook at night.

Even while holding onto the bed's railing, my body kept dropping down with a thud.

I saw the night ocean, coal tar-colored howling underneath the jet-black night, through the window of the cabin.

That was the savagery of the sea. That was the sea piercing the dream of the sea and bursting out. That was the paranoia of the sea.

All who had ever lived on this Earth, and all who were not living, were running toward Lady No, their hair, which had never been cut in their lives, shaken loose. Terrifying waves shook the boat up and down, up and down. The solar system might as well have been casting Earth out. The sea was in pain. Like the pain of giving birth to the devil's baby, like the pain of riding the devil's rhythm, it was the pain of giving up one's body to a grand rhythm. Lady No crawled through the hallways of the cargo hold and went to the service counter. "Please give me a pill to deal with this seasickness." Lady No learned from the attendants there that this boat was the only boat that had sailed out from the harbor that day. And because this boat was so big, nothing bad will happen, the attendants told her, so take the medicine and get some sleep, please. But when she returned to her room and glued herself to the window, Lady No shook like a crazy person and vomited every time she fell. They told her that she just had to submit her body to the rhythm of the waves, but her body refused.

The last of the gloom dissipated, and the jet-black night howled majestically in swirls. The dark universe arrived in front of Lady No and shouted at her. There was a great gesture. It rejected, rejected, rejected, rejected, and only rejected.

Only a single glass pane stood between Lady No and the universe of dark tar howling madly.

A lifeform shook in fear, draping itself in a cloak of all kinds of anxieties against this great and scary abstraction.

A little vortex called Lady No and a big vortex of the dark universe fought and rattled.

All that had once lived and faded and perished in this world, all their fates, cried out loudly.

Lady No thought how she will one day be this thing with hair shaken loose.

China was reached in the morning.

MIGRAINE

There is a forest inside my head.
One day a wind blows through that forest.
The same day when the forest shook my head.
The same day when people come with axes to cut down the trees of the forest.
On such a day, Lady No hugs her knees
And closes her eyes.

It seems as though no one lives in the forest
But there could be a person there, vaguely.
Is Lady No the refuge of this person? Prison? Hospital?
Is Lady No the material pain of a human residing in the place called the brain? Is she an insult?
Lady No gets more anxious the more this person curls up and burrows deeply within her.

Lady No gets acupuncture on her toes because of the pain in her head.
Because the trees in the forest are hurting,
Lady No is piercing their roots with needles.
May they find peace.

Lady No can't recognize the one who lives in the forest,
But the way the forest turns into a waste of grey,
And the way the forest floor is wet after rain,
And the way the old trees fell and were set aflame because of wildfire,
And the way that green leaves sprouted here and there,
She can sense these things easily.

Lady No constantly tries to have a conversation with the presence that lives in the forest of her head.

She greets that person who is armed with sensitive sensations with utmost respect.

That person stays there like a storm cloud who proves their existence with pain,

And Lady No sheds a branch of tears.

Lady No drinks hot tea.
Is the forest doing well?
Does the light reach there?
Is anyone getting lost in its paths?
The warm green liquid of the tea flows into the dark forest,
Asking how are you.

HUMILIATION

While sitting next to Lady No, he hits her chair.
He hits her chair while he speaks.
The body of Lady No shakes a little.
The vibration enters her body.
He hits her chair at the end of every sentence.
His sentences are short.
He hits to the beat.
The chair is the extension of Lady No.
First, it is the stomach of Lady No that vibrates to the beat.
Then it is her lungs.
Then it is her liver.
All the organs in the body of Lady No take turns to vibrate.
Lady No is listening to a percussion concerto in her body.
He is older than Lady No.
He is the teacher of Lady No.
He seems as though he has never despaired.
He wants Lady No to retract the opinion she just gave.
In Aerok, it is forbidden to publicly point out your teacher's behavior.
Lady No restrains herself.
She knows that everyone else sitting now in a circle is restraining themselves, and she does not want to spoil the mood.
The concerto in her body reaches the climax
Then he starts to hit even more.
Her body could explode in discord.
What he is saying is sophistry.
What he is saying is a self-excuse.
It is defending oneself by insulting others.
Lady No stands up.

"Teacher, please stop hitting this chair. I can hear our friendship breaking apart."

Men, ahjeossi, seniors, teachers, and elders rarely experience being turned into a percussive instrument.

The power they believe they have is a wall that cuts them off from their happiness and pleasure. Whether it came to them, whether they fought to earn it, whether they bled for it, whether it was prepared for them, the power they have is something they equip themselves with because they lack the confidence to look into themselves. So, they smell like fear and vanity. They smell of rot. That is what Lady No thinks. Whether they are inside a small circle or a big rectangle, Lady No thinks they would be happier with themselves if they were to throw it away.

Even when the body of Lady No gets away from the chair, her body vibrates like someone who has just gotten off a small boat.

It seems it will continue for several days.

THE ROLE ASSIGNED TO LADY NO IN THIS WORLD

A father and a son are walking on a path. The father tells his son, "Lift your head when you walk. A person is passing by." The person passing by is Lady No. She is one of those figures who appear when you read a script: Passerby 1, Passerby 2, Passerby 3. The passerby's role is to pass by. It is the role assigned to us in this city, to pass by. Lady No passed by like she was Passerby 4. Like a leaf falling on this wasteland of a universe. A leaf made a meek noise as it broke apart, but no one listened. Not even the leaf itself.

We live hanging on a tree called Seoul. Passerby 1 and Passerby 2 are far away. But then it strikes, the lightning of suffering. And then it descends, the thunderstorm that comes with fear. Smoke rises. Someone brings an axe to the trunk of our tree. We realize on the same day and hour that we are a community of shared fate, and we have all been hanging on to a corpse. A corpse that's been hanging on to someone else's hand. We end up knowing what we would be better off not knowing. When the subway train makes an emergency stop and the lights dim, we all look around our temporary abode, which is also the community of our shared fate. We are like people who have all fallen into the same well. And the eyes of Passerby 4 and Passerby 5 meet.

CONDUCTOR OF FATE

He is the conductor of screams.
He conducts the chorus of screams.

Unlike conductors of other orchestras,
He conducts from behind the chorus.
He has a particular affection for the scream of a soprano
And when the soprano screams the first phrase
Of a sharp aria and falls into her family's embrace,
He is in ecstasy.
It is because that is the sign for the alto, tenor, and baritone of the chorus to start making noise.
The longer this chorus singing goes on, the louder it is,
He succeeds.
And unlike other conductors, he enjoys conducting in secret.
Of course, there is no music sheet, but his conducting
Has a reputation.
None among us living has seen his face, nor will he ever see his face.
Lady No thinks every year that the music he conducted this year was the worst.

SHAKING MINARI

When spring comes, or at the very least, when the signs of spring come, I want to fill up a cart full of minari and wash them in the creek's cold water.

I won't mind if the creek's waters turn out to be so cold that they will turn my hands red. I want to dunk the green leaves inside the water and shake them.

It would be nice if there is a shower of rain.

It would be nice if I could hear the sound of a car passing by in the distance.

It would be nice if my hair gets drenched.

It would be nice if a black goat stands on the levee and stares at Lady No like she is a crazy woman.

All Lady No wants to do is to dunk the green leaves inside the water and shake them with abandon.

That is how she would like to wash away this cruel year that has just passed her by.

Like great silence. She wants to wash away the cruelty of time that camouflaged before us as if there was nothing inside it when it passed us by.

She wants to wash the trembling eyebrows of spring in the waters that are as clear as tears.

She wants to wash away the uncertainty that she had hidden in ice. She wants to come face to face with the world of fresh green almost overflowing her tray.

If they ask what she is doing, she will want to lift her eyes filled to the brim with her tears and answer, "I am washing minari!"

When the new spring comes.

TEACHER AND STUDENT

I have now lived longer as a teacher than as a student.
But the student within me will never disappear.

A teacher is, before anything else, someone who lives ahead of you.
She is the one who shows you life.
A teacher, in terms of shamans, is the body's spirit.
A teacher is, in the literal sense of these words, the one who lived ahead of you and died and came back. Meaning she is a ghost. Lady No is afraid that Lady No is a teacher.

Lady No will be the one who lives ahead of her student and be the first to die.
Lady No will be the one who will show them death.
Lady No has the duty to show them her bare-naked death.
But there lives within Lady No a student who will never disappear
So how did she ever become a grown-up called a teacher?
Lady No probably isn't qualified to be a teacher.
Perhaps the temperamental girl who lived and died before might have had a chance.
Winning an award for the first time is the same as this.
It means that you become someone who lived ahead of others and died before others.
Such a thought came to me after deciding who will win a certain award.

KAL

1

Father went missing.
Mom got married.
The eldest daughter was brought to live in Busan.
The son was brought to live in France,
And the younger daughter was brought to live in America.
The youngest hasn't been found yet.
The three siblings hugged one another at the airport.

The younger daughter brought a jacket she knitted for her brother to wear.
The younger daughter sang a song like a girl whose brother had turned into a swan.
"Clothes made out of thorns pierced me.
The sickle of Lord Moon pierced me, too.
The nail of Lord Star pierced me, too.
I sat on a chair of clouds spilling its cotton
And dyed the fabric with blood drops dripping from my swelling fingers."
The eldest daughter spoke, "I am sorry. I am truly sorry.
For sending you away to a distant land."

Changing into a jacket made of steel wires,
Knitted with blue fire,
The brother sang,
"I worked at a pig roasting farm
But I kept falling because I had no wings."

This is a shameful country.
This is a country that acts shamefully in fear of being shamed.

Why did Aerok tell these seven-year-olds, three-year-olds, barely one-year-olds,
To go and crawl the cement floors of foreign lands like naked snails?
Why did Aerok tell them to shudder and turn pale like frozen leaves of cabbages on market streets?

Why did Aerok tell them to leave like a toilet made from white wings
That gets covered with the shit of a flock of birds flying high?
The younger daughter sang,
"My house is made out of toilet paper.
When it rained, it could not protest
And got crushed into the ground."

When the airplanes bore her siblings far away,
The eldest daughter, left behind all alone, wept.

The runway was crowded with blue birds.

2

The adopted siblings said their farewells again at the airport as grown-ups.
Their conversation was only possible with triple interpretations.

After they left, the hypocrisy of Aerok remained like toilet papers,
The hypocrisy in which someone demands the humiliation of someone else.

Have you ever been on an airplane carrying babies flying away to foreign countries?
Have you ever gone on a vacation while listening to their cries?

OCTOBER

IDOLATRY BIBIMBAP

Even when we talk about poetry, we can't help but blabber idolatry. When I read writings about my country's poetry, there are times when it feels like I've eaten a bibimbap of sentences about other countries' poetry. On our works cited pages, it is difficult to find Aerok names. If the name of an Aerok person comes up, he is usually dead, or has stopped writing, or is someone who has become a legend because of his tragic life. When it is a foreign person who gets cited, then it is usually someone who is difficult to read in translation, or someone who has only just recently become known in Aerok as the latest fad. Our pitiful idols, they get their limbs sliced off and grafted together in Aerok's language. The reason we are constantly idolizing foreigners is perhaps because we have already prepared pedestals for worship and scorn within ourselves. Within poetry, the unfolding of ideology, the alibi of survival, the pathetic illusion known as nation, these are all idolatries. A poet feels with thinking, and thinks with feeling. There is nothing uglier than the pedestal that the poets enshrine within themselves. In the republic of poets, all are flat. Such thoughts came to me when I saw the names of foreigners and the dead among those listed when Aerok poets were asked to recommend the poets they honor and respect.

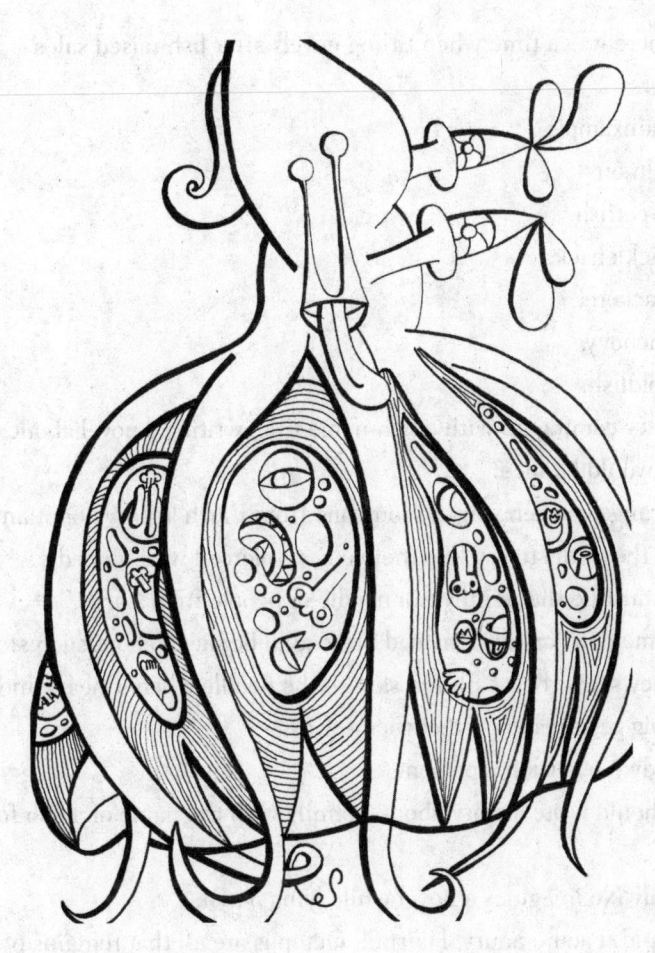

FISHES AND STORIES ABOUT FAMILIES

There was a time when titling novels after fish raised sales numbers.

For example,

Salmon,

Sweetfish,

Stickleback,

Mackerel,

Anchovy,

Goldfish.

After coming up with a fish-name title, writing a novel about a family would be nice.

Strangely, when you tell someone from Earth a story about any family, they start to cry like they've been pierced with a needle.

It must be that family is a needle to people from Earth.

Some don't cry and instead pretend to be mean about such stories.

They show their callused skin to the needle when it nears and make big gestures to protect themselves.

Lady No is such a person.

I should write a story about a family with the name of a fish for its title.

Lady No imagines a novel while lying down.

Squid, Pacific Saury, Hairtail, Octopus are all that remains of the fish still aviable to be used as titles of novels in Aerok.

Can Sea Cucumber or Sea Squirt work?

Would our parents permit it if they were to be reincarnated as fish in a novel? And so on.

THREE WOMEN

I met my three women friends for the first time in a while.
We talked about our recent lives.

Following is the summary of our talk:
Went insane.
Suspects something.
Went separate ways.
Aren't well.

In a world divided between the normal and the abnormal, our hours constantly fall towards the abnormal world.
And in the end, the world ends abnormally.
Where is normal love, and where is normal death?
Are we not demanding to be loved alone when we say "I love you"?

We shared our futures.
We shared endless catastrophes.
We speculated about our pasts and remembered our futures.

Thinking will die, hatred will soar, dreams will be shattered, and time will become abject, and humiliations will grow bigger, and surrender will have its final victory at last. Warmth will be stolen from our bodies.

Tubes stuck into our noses will force-feed us.
Covered in a transparent mask that will force us to breathe.
Underneath machines and rough hands.

I felt my heart was fully filled with gravel.

DAEHEUNG TEMPLE

A monk was hungry on a moon-bright night
Walking on a mountain
When tens of thousands of moons came out and asked him,
"Do you want to eat us? Do you want to eat us?"
Because he was hungry, he ate those moons all night,
Biting into them one by one and tearing them apart. (How out of breath he must have been.)
But then the morning came,
And the monk arrived at the temple,
And no one recognized who he was.
It was because he had grown so old over that single night,
As if he had aged a thousand years.
How many moons he must have eaten
For him to end up so.

On the night of the dark moon, it was so black that
We asked a self-proclaimed monk of debauchery, dressed in his ceremonial robes, to lead us.
In a single file, we held onto each other's sleeves and climbed toward the temple
On Duryun Mountain.
When the monk who was leading us, whose robe Lady No was holding tight,
Asked of her a song to guide them,
I made up a song as it came to me and sang it.
And the false monk said,
"Your words all end in metaphor
And symbolism."

So I said, "I hate those things more than anything else in the world," and

The monk of debauchery replied,

"If I don't have those things, I will die starving in this world

And get beaten to death in the next."

In the morning, I looked everywhere in the temple's kitchen

But I could not find the monk from the night before.

Because I did not see his face and only heard his voice, there was really no way to find him.

But I did hear during mealtime that there is a hermitage called Sungdoahm

Located south of the temple where apprentice monks meditate.

A spring there looks as though it was used for washing rice.

Once upon a time, from that hole of water, enough rice came out for a single meal each day.

But some monk stuck a stick in that hole, trying to get more rice to come out of there. Since then, only the water that looks as though it was used for washing rice comes out.

MY NAME AND YOUR NAMES

When someone in emergency says "Please save me," and
When someone calls on Lady No specifically to save them,

And, of course, when the name of Lady No is called,
My heart will tremble more.
And even if I might throw away my own life, I will get out of bed
To save the person behind that calling.
Because they shouted Lady No's name.

Barbara is a film about the name Barbara.
Barbara is an East German doctor, demoted to working in the countryside.
She asks a colleague to call their patients by their names.
Whenever those doctors call their patients by their names,
The details of each patient's life emerge.
It seems that the regime had erased the act of 'calling names."
When the patient calls her name saying, 'Barbara, please save me,'
She even gives up the chance to escape to the West for the patient's sake.

The name that Barbara calls doesn't just refer to a single person with the name of that patient.
The calling not only calls on someone's name but also shouts out and summons the vast continent of the other, or, of freedom.

Whether or not they lived or died in the whirlwind of a great war,
There is the name of someone who named their own story and presented it to the world, and

There is the name of a writer who covered up those names and copied those stories, and

There is the name of people who all died together in gas chambers. They all feel different.

Who is the one that exploited calling people's names?

Poetry and nation are antonyms.

A nation has the duty to call on each of its citizens' names, and poetry has the duty to place each of those names into silence.

WEDDING MARCH

Why is love always a diagonal line, always crossing paths?

Why are women on the stage willing to turn themselves into heroines of tragedy?

Why do women like to stand on that stage at that moment?

Have they fooled themselves into thinking that they will be able to pick happiness like picking the leaves off the branch of a tree?

Why do women direct their vengeance toward their children like Medea?

Will the skin get cut up and blood burst within themselves afterward?

The stage of misfortune that women are happy to step onto.

Even when they know that lights will go out.

Even when they know they will be peeling onions sprawled out next to a kitchen sink.

Why do they enter that stage?

Why do they put on the noose of the medal called sorrow?

Lady No thinks that the wedding march is the saddest song in the world.

After walking for a minute over a carpet where flowers are blooming, the princess of pure white is dethroned, buried beneath the applause of people in lines.

She will be a weeping woman in front of that abject thing called happiness, which she will never be able to catch.

She will incarcerate her heart.

And happiness is something drawn on the two-dimensional wedding invitation, therefore she will come to realize that a three-dimensional person like a woman can never have it. The paper main characters of doll plays will now be crumbled.

And she will forever collapse into being a Cinderella who prepares the hated table and never gets to wear her glass shoes.

She will be the bodhisattva of a thousand hands who will be the cleaning bodhisattva, cleaning up everything in and out of a house with all her hands.

And she will never return to that place before her eternal march of a single minute when she shone the brightest, because she desired neither trust nor love.

POET'S NAME

There are times when I am asked about whom I write poetry for.
Poetry is not written 'for' anything. Poetry can't be named with an object noun.

Poetry is spoken by the one who has forsaken their name.
A poet in a poem tries to get away from their name and become something that is frail and vast that can't be named.
(Who is that person, even when I call myself, I do not turn back to look at me.)

When the name of the one who writes poetry falls, the names that poetry has been calling come fully back to life at last.

There is that other place, the name of which has been erased.
That dark place where an 'I' who has lived in this world disappears,
Feeling as though one has arrived at a time when no one will remember who 'I' was.
This endless ventilation of calling for that time to arrive. This anxiety of the one who stays inside that time.
That place where I can no longer recognize 'I.' That place where 'I' is not a first-person point of view.
That place where 'I' is a six-person and a seven-person point of view.
That place where even matter is an illusion.
I look for 'I' in the shades of purgatory. Who is this, in this place where 'I' can no longer recognize 'I'?

The 'I' of the poem is a designation for a certain crack between 'I' and what is 'not I'. Born under a name but having lost the name, one discovers 'I' after what happens. Pieces of lost experience. Ruins. Dust. An 'I' who cannot be called an 'I' walks through such a thick fog.

The world of desire that 'I' do not know but only through sensations. The world where the name is erased like cumulus clouds changing their shapes every moment.

An act of ventilating nothingness into the world of names. The secret of silence. The parade of absence. The oblivion of a certain world finally made beautiful when it takes off its name. The ecstasy of absence.

Of the gestures of hands building that frail yet infinite and unbound world.

LADY NO'S WIFE

Night deepens and
A hungry bird chirps powerlessly and
Dry leaves still hang on to their branches and rustle and
Rats in darkness wait for their chance
On this eerie night.

Someone sits Lady No on a table
And places a white napkin on her and

Makes soup and
Salts it to taste and
Slices fruit and
Minces meat and
Lets the smell fill the air and
Like a nanny filled with the kindness of a gentle wife
Checks on Lady No in secret to make sure she is eating and
Checks whether Lady No is smiling and
Is happy and
I hope there is someone who takes an interest in me like that.
I hope Lady No will have a wife
Such as her once in her life.
This hungry evening when I don't even want to place a spoon on the table.
The evening when I eat a dinner of fancy.

DEATH METAL AND AN ORPHAN GIRL

After it snowed for a few days,
Death Metal went to meet an orphan girl and
They walked the snowy path together.
The girl was tiny
And wore a red coat and a white cap.
The girl was like a red cherry on a snow-white street
Or like a red light,
Being careful.
Death Metal next to the girl didn't know how to walk
Or how to open his mouth
Or how to face this air and let it in.

So they walked without even holding hands.
Death Metal spoke to the orphan girl who wore a pink skirt that seemed to be made of thin ice.
"What do you like?"
The orphan girl replied,
"Not anything."

On the street without the sun,
On the street whipped by the cold,
Death Metal said to the girl,
"You are my heart,"
And the orphan girl spoke,
"Why does a heart live in an orphanage?"

And a father and a daughter had no place to go
But walked, looking for where to go.

A SPINE CALLED SOLITUDE

 Wearing a red windbreaker swollen like a balloon, his head covered in a beanie,
  He walks alongside the Han River.
  He walks for four hours every day.
  When he meets Lady No, he speaks.
  "For poets, solitude is their spine.
  I live, stuck in that spine.
  From my spine, poetry comes."
  Wearing a windbreaker filled with red wind, he
  Walks like an arrow that left its bow.
  He passes by like a red beast
  That appears on a cold winter day near the shores of the Han River.
  He walks past, mumbling poetry.
  He mumbles and walks, he whose throat was branded as a poet long ago in divine punishment.

WHY DO OLD PEOPLE BECOME CHILDREN?

Because, having lived, there's not much to it.
Because that much has passed by.
Because there is no reason to live like a grown-up.
Because living like a grown-up has led to regrets.
Because even youth has been transcended.
Because of confusion about how I have become someone that isn't me.
Because it turns out I wanted to be someone that isn't me.
In the waiting room of an orthopedic clinic,
A grandmother sang a song she sang as a child with a tiny voice
While shaking her leg.
I wondered if she had dementia, but she received her treatment well, talked to nurses, and asked for directions to the pharmacy.
And then, she was talking to another grandmother sitting next to her.
Like all the elderly folks of Aerok, they didn't introduce themselves with names but checked each other's ages first and conversed about their fear of death.
While they talked, it seemed as if they weren't acknowledging the existence of each other. Each one seemed to talk about only herself.
Their expressions were stricken with fear.
So why do old people become children?
Probably because they fear being alienated from the future.
They are already alienated from the past, so there is no guarantee that they won't be alienated from the future.

The hanja character 老 (old) looks like a child with long hair, someone with the special right to host a god.

It looks like a person who has gotten nearer to a god without realizing that they are hosting a god.

And yet why do old people become children?
Because our souls have always been children.

WHAT IS INSPIRATION

A student spoke,
"I can't find inspiration, so I don't think I will be able to do this assignment."
Truly, it's been such a long time since I heard the word inspiration.
That's right. There is no poem as good as the one before it is put into words.

Poetry is written when 'I' am staying in another state of being.
Poetry leads 'I' into another state of being.

Poetry is found in a different world called the poetic condition.
Of course, the catalyst for divulging is usually moral indignation or existential alienation,
And the procedure of imagination is often political.
That indignation, that alienation, that hope leads 'I'
To be in another state of being.

Poetry is the unfolding of another being
And sinking into another state.
It is the shouting of stillness.
Inspiration is the answer one gives when they have heard the words of the other called 'I',
It is the impossibility of that answer.

That is why after a poem has been finished,
It is only right that the 'I' in the poem disappears.
After drinking it all up, there remain bits of 'I' in the glass.
It would be fortunate if I could leave behind just enough of 'me' as the remnants needed to cast a fortune.

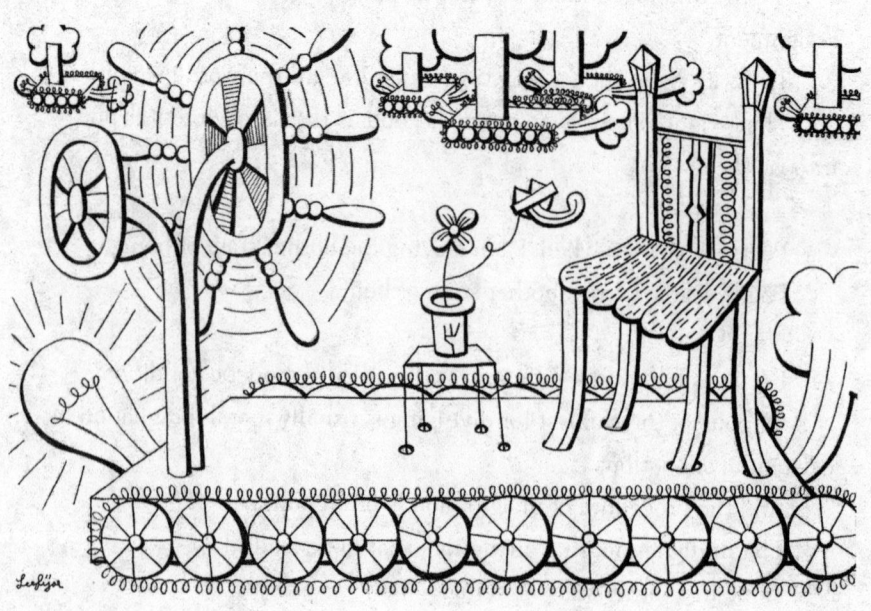

IF ONLY I HAD A CONSOLE, TOO

    A small whirlwind brushing past one's heart.
    A bright branch of lightning striking one's head like an electric hammer.
    A poetic phrase as sharp as the killing edge of an iron
    That came from the hand of Lady No and went all the way to Mars
in a flash.
    If only there were a machine that could store all such things.
    For example, something like how you install a set of drums in a room
    With high ceilings and surround it with mics and start
    Jamming and mixing voices and the sounds of instruments together.
    A vivid sound.
    A transparent chord where no one can hide.
    If only a studio with recording gear were available to poets
    Where bass, guitar, and drum sounds could be smooshed together
    Without gaps using a Neve console.
    If there were a record console with tens of thousands of buttons
    That could mix the rhythm and the music and a sigh
    And wind them up to surge toward the universe,
    Then we wouldn't have to do such boring labor as trying to capture
words with a pen.
    We could let go of this dreadful poverty and properly
    Forget about this little thing called poetry.
    If only Lady No could have such a console.

WHAT IS MY BODY MADE OUT OF

When our bodies arrived in this world for the first time, perhaps when our shapes were being formed during pregnancy,

When our brains were being formed, our hearts made, our toes dividing,

Did we sense sounds and smells and shapes separately?

Sensations back then were probably not yet divided for us, still a singularity.

In dark water, the five senses of each of our mothers, smooshed into a single thing, probably this then became our bodies.

It must have been that we had a unified sensation in which the sound that came from outside our moms' bodies became shapes, and the sound that came from within our moms' bodies became functions!

While we kept our eyes closed and our fists tight, there must have been a mechanism in which our bodies were made.

Like an orchestra, the moms' sensations must have swarmed to the fetus like reality made by dreams.

The auditory as the piano

The visual as the violin

The taste as the cello

The tactility as the clarinet

The smell as the trombone

And this symphony flooding us became our arms sometimes and became our toes sometimes.

And sometimes our liver and sometimes our kidneys.

The heart must have begun as a drum as tiny as a fingernail floating on water.

The sound ripening into a whole body.

There must have been a world where sensation was one.

There must have been a factory where sensation was the world.

LEVIATHAN OF LADY NO

A dove flies and crashes into the window of a car.
There is a loud noise.
But the dove flies away still.
It must at least have gotten a concussion.

You keep going, and you encounter a dead cat or a dead dog that was run over.
While driving on mountain roads, you meet a deer with its intestines hanging out.

For a few days, when you pass by the same place, you see the face of the dead cat.
Like a bad thought you had forgotten, you come across the dead body of the cat.

Like a single dog can make tens of thousands of birds in Eulsook Island fly at once,
Lady No is a dormant leviathan.

Lady No unzips the zip that goes all the way down from her back to her waist and brings out her leviathan.
It slogs-slogs out.
It comes out until it feels the world.

Lady No zips herself up again and goes back on her way.

ARROGANT LORD ENGLISH

After the poetry reading is over, an American student asks a question.

"Have you ever thought about writing poems in English?"

Lady No answers,

"No."

I don't want to give the student a generous answer.

Because this is America.

Because Lady No is reading poems at a college where they are paying tuition.

I want to ask if they have ever seen a poet writing in two different languages, but I stop myself.

One language is its own world, its own universe. Don't you know that? I want to ask this but stop myself.

For instance, Lady No is someone who despairs every day

At the boundlessness of language as she scratches at the surface, with her pen's tip,

Of the language of Aerok that is as wide and deep as an ocean.

When a poet's fate is to dedicate their writing life to digging into the universe of Aerok's language—a foreign language, you say?

Lady No would like to answer the student, 'I have so many things to say other than No!'

Isn't it the case that Americans don't like to hear or listen to language that isn't English?

Isn't it the case that they don't even like to read translated fiction?

Lady No wants to stereotype Americans like others have done before her, but she stops herself.

And shouts, "Next question, please."

After the reading, an American teacher speaks.

"When Aerok writers who know some English come to America for readings and Q&As, I prefer that they don't use English at all. We have professional interpreters, so there is no reason for that. In the country of Aerok's language, poets rank higher than presidents, don't they?

When such poets end up saying some low-level words in English, it makes them look bad, you know." Oh, you are an arrogant piece of work, Lord English.

OLD DAUGHTERS

"It's a relief that my mom is dead,"
a friend tells me at her mother's funeral.
"If she had left us a little earlier, then I would have been free earlier,"
a friend says, dressed in funerary clothes.

"My mom is dead, and now I am a free person,"
said Walter Benjamin.
Right after returning from his uncle's funeral, Fernando Pessoa, who was an orphan, expressed,
"That soft and light sensation of liberation."
"One day in February, as if to bless the letters you and I have been exchanging (about death), my mother passed away at age 83," wrote Ayako Sono to her priest, found in the book of her letters that was published, which now anyone can read.

What is freedom in such cases?
What is blessing in such cases?

The fruits from the tree twist their skinny stalks
and fall, saying, "It is my turn now."
They fall one or two at a time.
They fall faster during a storm.

As if they wanted to return to where they were hanging from,
the unseen seeds of peaches
shout from inside the bodies of peaches.
"What a relief that Mom is dead."

Fall is coming at full speed.

THE PEACEFUL REIGN OF KING SENTIMENTAL THE GREAT

To succeed as an artist in Aerok, you must first enter into the peaceful reign of sentimentalism.

You must begin by getting eyes moist a little.

To get eyes moist, you must follow family, people, and nation—in that order—

While handling the issues of their injuries, healings, and wounds.

Aerok's romanticism mobilizes Aerok's sentimentalism by invoking the nation and the people.

In Aerok, the biggest praise might very well be when people say that your art work reached their hearts or made them weep.

Mysticism or sentimentalism can be an insult to art itself, or to those who dwell in it.

Sentimentalism does not require sensitivity.

Sensitivity is the deepening of a soul of a person who has achieved death and absence.

Sentimentalism only wants to look at tragedy but does not want to experience it.

Sentimentalism gives itself to the torture of hope, on its own volition, and weeps in pain. It is the sewer of romanticism. It is the gesture that seeks to seduce people to a house of illusion called their heart.

Sentimentalism is the stealthy disguise of hollow desire. It is the proof of a worthless soul.

It is the narcissism of one who refuses, to the very end, to give up on a self they cannot even be sure exists.

It is the lament of one who has given up creativity after letting emotion take the place of literature.

Sentimentalism is the indulgence that precedes thinking.

Those who indulge in it are far away from the work that remains silent in stillness and endures suffering.

Those who indulge in it never let go of the reader's nervous system and tear ducts.

Sentimentalism is a curtain cast with emotion that does not allow us to reach the nucleus of what happened, only lighting its borders. It is the net that lets us fall so that we become an audience of the curtain.

Asking one to give up sentimentalism may be like asking one to give up the trophy called readers.

Mixing sentimentalism with nationalism or any national event works really well.

S/he will become a respected intellectual and their house will become a site of pilgrimage.

S/he will have earned it by swearing loyalty to the peaceful reign of King Sentimental the Great, receiving it as a medal.

There were people who made us uncomfortable with their work and ran away from the mysticism that was coming for them.

Is it a failure of life when such people disappear, isolated, after rejecting solidarity with the sentimental?

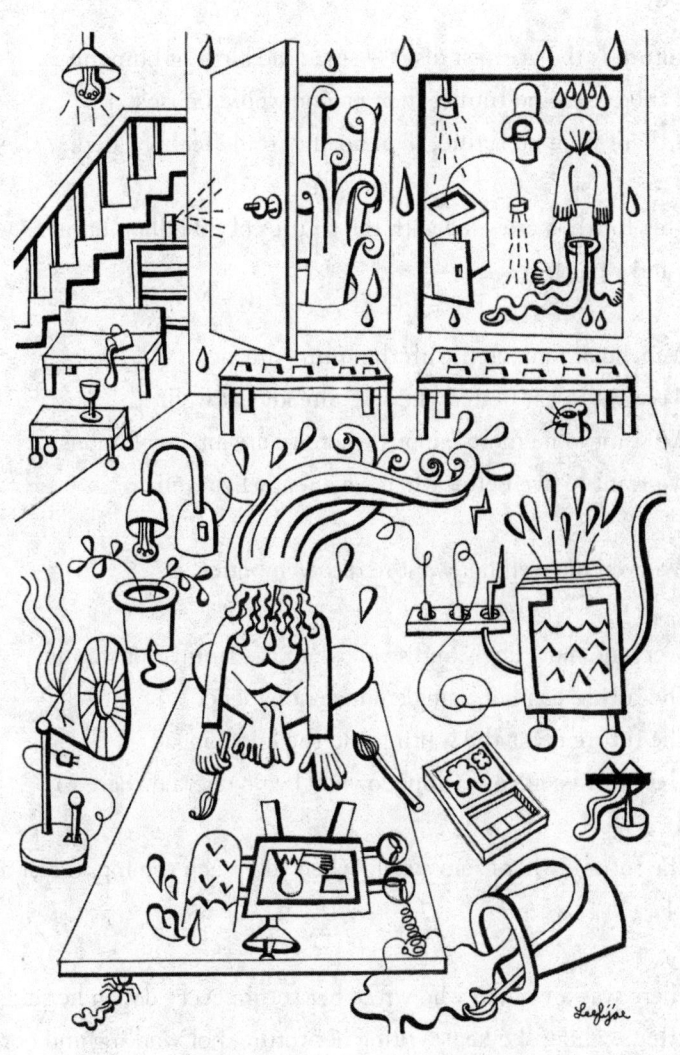

INFECTED WITH FUTURE

Future is the greatest disease since the birth of humanity.
If there were no future, then no one would be sick.
If there were no future, then no one would feel cheated.

This Earth is crowded with the futures of 80 billion humans who came and went.

We who are infected with the future are sick.
We want to eat better when we already eat well.
We want to be more famous when we are already famous.
We want to live better when we already live well.

We even die well but want to die even better.

Everyone must chew and swallow up the future constantly.
The future has not a single ounce of patience.
The future owns the waiting and the knocking.
The future comes crashing, owned by no one, nowhere to be found.
The future, where zero awaits when you reach the top as fast as possible.

There was a woman who wrote her future every day in her diary.
After a while, she kept writing her future, not working and not sleeping.
She made more money, became more beautiful, stood on bigger stages,

even fabricated her academic resume, hired a contract killer to kill someone,
and went to prison. Her handbags and her desks
were brimming with the futures she wrote down with a pencil on any piece of paper that came to her.

FEBRUARY ZOMBIE

Among those who live in temperate regions, it is rare to find anyone who says that February is their favorite month.

It is a pitiful season stuck between winter and spring.

It is a season when you run your fingers through your thickly matted hair that grew long during the college entrance exam period, which isn't even finished yet.

But it is a season when you feel sunshine that is a little different from winter's.

Lady No looks through the bus window and watches the people outside.

Disheveled faces looking like animals coming out from hibernation.

The people of the northern hemisphere look their ugliest in February.

They look like people who can no longer wait for what they have been waiting for.

Having been ordered to go back to the living world right after arriving at purgatory, these people stand around like they are waiting for the return train.

On the faces of these people remain exhausted sighs of the ones who endured the long winter's death, and also the elegies for lifeforms that live only for a year.

We don't live only for a year, but on each of our faces, there lingers an exhaustion that might as well have come from having lived through an entire cycle of life.

If it is the case that we didn't die this passing winter, then how is it that our memories are so faint? Lady No sighs while looking out the window of her bus.

Outside the window are faces of those who have certainly passed through death.

They are all glued hard to the ground.

Houses and trees and airplanes are all glued hard to the ground.

GENRE OF SERVILITY

When I am riding the subway, the first thing I receive is "do not" orders.

After a while, I receive "report this and that" orders.

And after another while, I start receiving "beware of" orders. There are "mind your manners" and "be careful" orders, too.

Warnings repeat endlessly.

And pretty soon, I get broken in, starting to feel like I need to say yes, yes.

I open a book to ignore these kinds of sounds

And suddenly a man throws a piece of paper atop my pages.

His paper is filled with a confession about his life.

He demands money now that he has confessed.

This particular genre of writing has its own rules.

First, an A4 sized piece of paper needs to be cut in half, and the penmanship needs to be zigzagged.

Everything from birth to handicap to illness needs to be written down.

A tragedy that has befallen a good family must be presented.

Of course, the crime syndicate that actually wrote this for their beggars and forced them out to beg must not be seen.

The frightening violence behind these words must be covered up.

And that is how the genre of servility is completed.

A moneybag hangs on the beggar's stomach.

His speech is long but his words get rolled back into his mouth.

The passengers in the subway car do not listen to his words.

With a microphone in his hand, he says, "This is where I am going."

We are now passing Dongjak Station and now we are passing Yichon Station.

The speechmaker with a basket in his hand walks slowly through the middle of a subway car.

A politician makes a speech on a podium installed on top of a truck.

Above the politician's head, a placard with his name on it waves in the wind.

They are the people who pollute our skies and walls the most, writing their names.

They are the people who cause the worst noise pollution, shouting their names.

They beg us and then they oppress us.

They steal our money and drive around with it in their trunks.

No pedestrian wants to stop and hear their speech about how Aerok is diseased somewhere.

His speech also follows the rules of the genre of servility.

The speechmaker moves onto the next crossroad like the speechmaker of the subway.

People at last becoming givers of orders after having begged for so long.

People get broken into their own erect bodies that they built up with their writing. Their saliva drenches their sleeves like rain.

LADY NO DOES NOT WANT TO BE MARKED

Lady No leaves a movie theater.
She leaves the theater as if she is coming back from a journey to another world and is now closing the door to it.
I think about the people living in movie theaters. I think about the people who live inside the screen, eternal and imperishable.

People who live without eating. People who live for decades, without ever changing their clothes.
People who look at people who came after them, playing music composed by men from an earlier century. People who look at their descendants with square eyes that are white like screens. Those are the people who live there. People who wear sunglasses at night, from the ruins of Detroit to the alleys of Tangier, traveling toward night and night only. Even though all this happens only in their films, there was an awfulness called eternity in them. Lady No leaves the theater. After crossing the street, Lady No looks back. And tries to let them go from her thoughts. But it feels like someone is living out the life of Lady No in a film. It feels like someone is living as Lady No though Lady No is no longer of this world. It even feels like someone is making love that should have been the love of Lady No. Immortal for hundreds of years. The duty of a lifeform that lives only because it is alive—enduring, being Lady No and at the same time Lady No's descendant—that ennui of a single human being, has been passed down to Lady No. Poor Lady No.
Lady No watches the same movie three times.
It is just a vampire movie.

For two hours in a theater seat, Lady No feels like Lady No's blood is getting sucked dry.

Simone de Beauvoir's *All Men Are Mortal* and Virginia Woolf's *Orlando* take as their main characters a person who won't and/or can't die for hundreds of years. They write about their misfortunes. Women writers teach us that 'what you should be most happy about being born in this world is that you are slated to disappear in the future.' Why do certain women writers like to write about these immortal misfortunes? Yet such women writers are now happily dead.

HOSPITAL WARD

A very young nurse who came into the hospital ward asked my very old father,
"How many years have you been smoking cigarettes?"
"Fifty years before I quit."
"Ah ha!"
"How many years have you been drinking alcohol?"
"Seventy years."
"Ah ha!"
The nurse's eyes kept getting bigger,
As if they were looking into the abyss of a well.
"How is your sex life?"
"No interest."
"Ah ha!"
"Are you depressed?"
"Always."
"Ah ha!"
Both Mom and Lady No are shocked,
By the fact that there is depression within her father.
That there is emotion within him.
"How many minutes do you walk per day?"
"I don't like to walk."
"Ah ha!"
We pretended to not see an old man sharing his story for the first time,
While watching him with every bit of our energy.
We had never asked Father any such questions,
But the nurse seemed as though she was standing before an abyss,
The depth of which she could not know.
"Ah ha!"

I felt like a stone falling down a deep well.

IF THERE ARE REALMS FOR EACH PART OF SPEECH

Mental illness, after all, is probably something that arises from spending too long dwelling in the domain of adverbs, that space where adjectives proliferate.

And frenzy, or its leftover sediment called sorrow, too, probably arises from lingering too long in that domain where adverbs and adjectives dwell together.

Life described as being healthy probably belongs to nouns.

What people believe is normal is located within the realm of nouns.

A life that does not look back at adverbs or adjectives and only looks at nouns.

Parts of speech other than nouns may all be pointing toward hallucinations.

Only when a postpositional particle is added to a noun does the noun soften. Michel Serres called prepositions angels.

However, poetry endlessly postpones naming of names. It endlessly activates images to make the noun fall.

In other words, adverbs and adjectives point toward the energy,

And verbs point toward the energy's movement, charging toward the other side of rationality.

However, poets and physicists are people who see even matter as energy. People who see even nouns as adjectives and adverbs.

People who are doing the work that has nothing to do with survival. People who keep placing next to verbs adverbs of madness. People playing with parts of speech who mistake madness and revolution as the same thing. Therefore, Lady No's anxiety deepens every day.

When a noun gets carried out from a house, another noun claims that house.

And then, many different parts of speech come and live together in that house again.

Some get diagnosed as being normal, and some go crazy.

This changing of positions happens every day though they are not the meaning of the world, nor the subjects of the world.

We call them poets whose syntactic abilities tend toward adjectives and adverbs.

Borges's Tlön is a country without nouns.

It is a country that believes that the universe is a kind of mental process.

THE PLACE NOW

There is an 'absence' that overtakes us faster than light.
That moment when 'Lady No' is captured by 'absence.'
The absence of 'Lady No' will expand beyond the universe.

Like the moment when the present of 'Lady No' disappears,
The death of 'Lady No' will also overtake her faster than light.

Poets suffer from nostalgia for absence.
Because of this nostalgia for that place from before their birth,
They suffer anxiety, depression, ennui, and loneliness.

'Lady No' visits a doctor and speaks to him. I am anxious.
I feel a whoosh at the center of my body.
The doctor answers her.
Anxiety signifies a 'condition.'
Does that mean 'Lady No' is a condition?
The doctor answers that 'Lady No' is a state.

Poetry exfoliates 'I' from 'I' and makes it a 'you,' makes it a 'thou.'
The frequency of that exfoliation makes 'Lady No' fall into anxiety.
Anxiety exfoliates 'Lady No' from 'Lady No.'
'Lady No' becomes endlessly distant from 'Lady No.'

If an infection runs rampant that will not allow humanity to reproduce on Earth,
Leading us to stuff infected people into sacks and bury them
Like the way we bury ducks and chickens infected with flu.
And if the last human left on Earth disappears.
And if only the rats left on overgrown open fields prosper.

And if the rats point to themselves and declare that they are the lord of all creatures.

And if one remembers Earth from beyond the space being held at the kingdom of 'absence.'
Then 'absence' will be infinite while keeping the nostalgia about Earth.

We must be living within such infinity.
This is the only explanation for why oblivion comes to us so quickly.

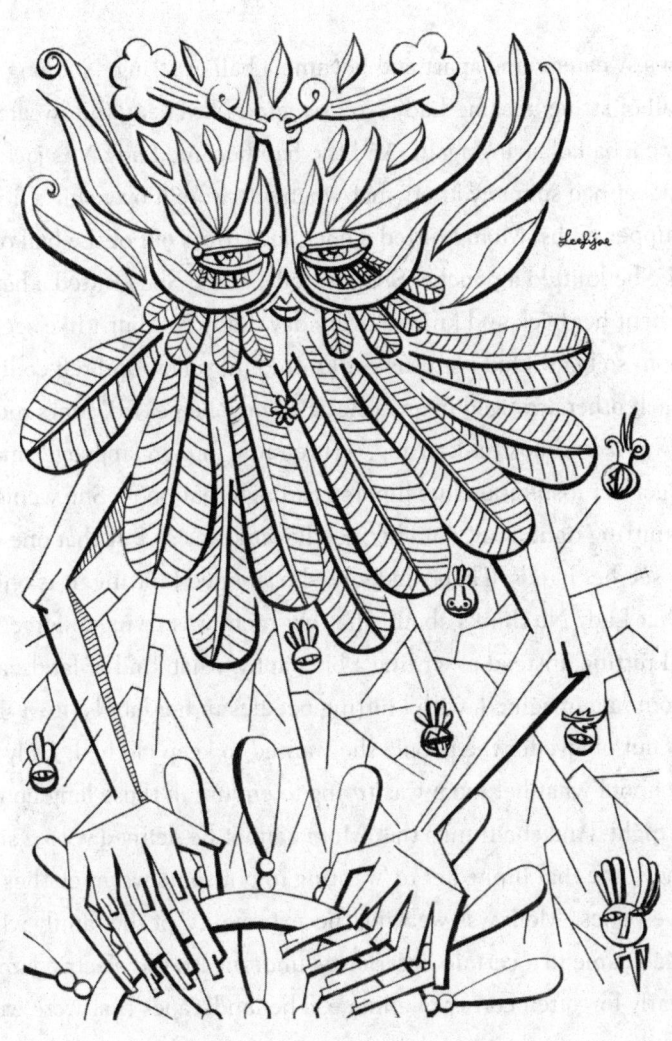

MOM'S KNITTING

Father's sweater came apart and became a ball of string. Not long after, the ball of string became Lady No's sweater. Next year, the sweater became a ball of string again. And the ball became Lady No's jacket. The jacket had so many knots that when you wore it over shirts, it hurt one's upper limbs. Mom knitted a one-piece dress out of the ball of string. She knitted a poncho. She knitted a scarf. She knitted a hat. Mom bent her back and knitted every day. Lady No didn't like seeing her mom so bent. Odd patterns got knitted in, yellow and red coiling into each other arranged in an ecstatic color scheme. In Mom's room, there was a textbook for knitting, written in a foreign language, and Mom got her inspiration just flipping through that book. She would start knitting right away. And her needlework was so fast that one could barely see her hands. Then suddenly, she stopped knitting. It is only now that Lady No thinks about what her mom was trying to forget while knitting, instead of writing a biography, what kind of landscape her mom had imagined, with knitting needles in her hands. It wasn't simply out of love for the people she wanted to keep clothed. Lady No thinks about what her mom was trying to endure in those long hours of the night. And she thinks that Mom cannot be defined with a single sentence, one that limits her to 'wanting to put some warm clothes on her loved ones.' Mom was weaving the 'externality' of the family while daybreak came to a certain 'interiority' underneath the electric lamp of the nearly forgotten corner of a home. The landscapes that were woven as they disappeared into each knit, the narratives that hovered about a crumbling Mom.

Until the arrival of what Sylvia Plath called 'the daybreak, every daybreak when the hour arrives and the effect of sleeping pills dissipates'.

EPILOGUE

ENNUI

I am suspicious if Lady No is Lady No, if what Lady No perceives is what Lady No is perceiving, if the life Lady No is living is what Lady No lives. Is Lady No in fact living out the life of Lady No, or could it be that Lady No has crushed herself besides a life? Lady No is sitting in front of her desk like a pilot who has parachuted down in an emergency from a strange place. Nothing is new. God has a great obsession with patterns. Are not Universe, Time, and Life all patterns? Why are God's patterns always variations on the same?

Perhaps thinking is synonymous with imprisonment. Perhaps the more you think, and the more doors you open, the more you see of the prison. Isn't thinking no more or no less than feeling the guard approach you in the prison of irrationality?

This feeling of being imprisoned on this Earth, in a vast prison called Aerok, after all other lifeforms have gone extinct. This feeling of an eternal universe that will never die, of being in an eternal stasis. This feeling of spinning the bicycle wheel as hard as one can but being stuck in the same place. This feeling of waking up early in the morning and working until late but realizing that such labor is meaningless. This feeling of adding "No" or "Not" to every verb or noun, and then sitting down. This feeling of all the components within and without one's body being composed of ennui. A feeling that every part of me, inside and out, is made up of ennui. A sense that the world itself consists of a white substance called ennui—a sea of ennui, a sky of ennui, and a wind of ennui, all cast forth by the demise of a white giant.

Yet, seized by the nothingness that hides its face in this ennui, I find myself longing to be hurled into the realm of the impossible. I even wonder if, within this ennui, there might be a kind of martyrdom in casting myself into infinity.

MUSIC'S EXISTENCE

When I am listening to music, I think about another world.

A place where there are high and low parts, and the whole.

A place where there are swelling waves composed of counterpoints, harmonics, and melodies.

A place that is infinite but ephemeral.

Lady No listens to music while at a lecture.

Lady No doesn't like people speaking from the podium.

There are times when Lady No must go up to the podium and provide words of affirmation.

Those are the moments when I would like to evaporate.

I look at Lady No who is now at the podium holding her fists tight. Stupid. Pathetic. Ignorant.

Listening to music, let's imagine a tree with blossoming yellow flowers.

Yellow brass instruments fill the world with different waves.

Singing smoke puffs out from the chimney, its world expands endlessly.

The face of the one who speaks from the podium looks like they are wearing a stainless mask.

The stainlessness flows down toward the faces of the people who have gathered before her.

In a single moment, Lady No explores a world that has cast out language.

I try to reconstruct a world within myself that has sunk into rhythm.

When Lady No imagines the waters of the valley that is flowing once again

She feels like she is drowning.

Lady No keeps her bleary eyes open and frolics in the other world that exists somewhere in this conference room.

Trees and flowers and waves and winds and landscapes all possess their own time and rhythm.

The seeds, the times, the landscapes play their own instruments within themselves.

Rhythms are mixing. Crashing. Harmonizing.

From the music's bright light, I look out across the stainless space.

The music has fulfilled the duty of time within time.

The lecture is nearing its end.

EARTH-SMELLING KEYSTROKES

Lady No crossed the border. A smell was blowing in a town that everyone had abandoned, on his piano, in his mumblings. Lady No wrapped herself with his place as if it were a coat, and she was ruled by his smell. And Lady No knew. That there was music remaining alone on a land where none remained. That there was a person who built a transparent house of air by knocking on air. That there was someone who shook the earth. That the mumbling loneliness of the one who endured this place all his life was still blowing on these streets, his specific fingers striking the keys. How the musical notes that went through him stayed in the air. How they touched the floor. How they fell on the windows like rain, giving hearts their slight trembles. Lady No felt all. The movements of his fingers. Whenever she heard that sound, she would recognize him even in a dream. Even if she was far away, she would shout, 'Those are his keystrokes.' The smell of earth, the smell of air, the level of humidity. The smell of clouds came from the movement of his fingers. His fingers buoyed by them. Those fingers kept before them the infinity of the outside and fell into the infinity of the inside. The infinity fell on its own as if something got stolen from it by his incessant piano playing. In poetry, like music, there are such keystrokes. That is, the poet's own movement of her fingers. There are poets whom we can identify even after covering up their names, just by listening to their rhythms. Lady No recognizes his music that plays this landscape. The transparent music, the music that has sealed within itself the sound of what is inside ice. The music that makes us shudder because once it sprouts it will never go back. The music that will make us say, 'It won't get off me!' So, start playing right now. When Lady No arrived at the pianist's hometown, his piano performance was like a hallucination that would not leave her. There was no way to prove it, but I thought that the feeling of this landscape, the landscape of this feeling, created his finger's movements. And that the landscape, like a healing wound, was probably what squeezed him.

THE ROOMMATE OF LADY NO

Back when Lady No was working for a publisher,

The government censored all the newspapers, books, magazines, and journals printed in her country.

Whenever she brought copies of a manuscript to City Hall,

Soldiers in uniforms, sitting at their desks as if they were the ones working at a publishing house, censored the manuscripts of poets and writers.

They painted dark tar over words and pages deemed unpublishable, then gave them back to Lady No.

It was impossible to know why certain words had been erased. Like how certain songs got banned in Aerok, only the censors knew the reasons. Faster than the number of books that were being published, countless varieties of reasons were being produced every day.

For example, some common reasons for censoring a work were that the work was degenerate, that it made fun of soldiers, that it used certain words like freedom, and that it wasn't allowed to cite this or that other work.

Lady No didn't even cry when she returned from picking up the manuscripts that had gone through the censors, but she cried when she had to go and hand the authors their tarred books and tell them why.

When she went to see the economist R on his deathbed, who had hoped to see the last work of his life in print, she had to declare the death of his book before the dying author. He wants to see his book published before he dies, the economist's wife told Lady No on behalf of her husband.

Without saying anything, the economist wept on his deathbed.

Behind his thin, wrinkly glasses, his tears flowed down to his ears.

There were times when Lady No had to manage the publications of plays to coincide with the plays' opening nights. There were times when she had to manage the publications of novels.

There was a time when Lady No was the bearer of news regarding the deaths of books.

In Aerok's city hall, there was a dark publisher, and they only kept dark coal tar in their office.

There were days when everyone who lived in Aerok was sinking into the quagmire of irrationality. There were days when people who lamented in the castles of sorrow spilled out into the streets like wind. There were days when days were only grey. There were days when the dream within a dream was put down under the light of censorship.

Lady No was a colorless, scentless, nameless editor of lowest rank at her publisher. No one would have known if someone had slapped her face. She wept into her blankets, wondering why the days were always grey. She was an editor who was submitting the poems she wrote without anyone knowing.

A story once expressed can no longer be possessed by anyone.

This story lives on in the country of stories. The life of Lady No is separate from the life of the story.

Within Lady No there is a well-organized pile of stories and gestures from that time that have yet to soar out of her. Like dormant volcanoes.

THE SHOES YOU WEAR WHEN YOU ENTER YOUR DREAMS

Why do people take off their shoes when they choose to die?

Shoes lie on the bridge, as painful and horrifying as an undressed body.

Looking like the meeting of an unfamiliar 'I' on an unfamiliar street.

Looking like an 'I' surprised at seeing 'I' in the mirror.

Some shoes grow old faster than Lady No.

Where are all the different pairs of shoes that Lady No dragged with her all her life?

Will they be the shoes that she wears when she enters her dreams?

Do the shoes you've abandoned in life return as the shoes you wear when you enter the factory of dreams?

Will this world also abandon Lady No?

Lady No trudges along like someone else's pair of shoes.

She trudges along, left foot right foot, as if she is already something someone is wearing as they enter their dreams.

FASTING

For eleven days,
Contrary to rumors,
I didn't crave a thing.
Later, I didn't even want water.
But the sky's film kept peeling away, layer by layer.
All day long, Lady No peeled away
That blue film rolled like an egg
Until she stopped.
It seemed that even a lifetime of peeling wouldn't be enough
So I asked for a sip of thin gruel
Like a drifting cloud.
On the eleventh day, even without forecast,
Hot drizzle fell.

POET'S AFTERWORD

These writings and drawings were originally serialized on the internet over a period of eight months under the title 'Master of Loneliness Master of Ennui'. (To be precise, it wasn't really eight months. The serialization ceased for 7 weeks by 7 days, for a total of 49 days. Days during which it was shameful to be alive. My soul was so ashamed that I could not endure it.)

I did not reveal my name when I started this serialization, and I didn't reveal it when it ended. Whenever one of my readers figured out who I was, I asked them not to spoil it for the others. I wanted the comments that came after my internet-posted words to be unrelated to myself, to be read as words that belong to that space only.

I wanted to achieve transparent poetry. This desire deepened every day, and I often had out-of-body experiences, times when I looked at myself blankly. These experiences led to invasions from anxiety and loneliness and ennui that took turns to find me. Suffering in this terrible cycle, something appeared before me, as if for the first time. Something that had volume but had no weight. A smell that had abandoned its body. Something that was like a sound. Something that was already a ghost.

Now, I think I can call it poetic genesis, that act of looking at myself after abandoning my body. When this other called poetic genesis suddenly soars out of my body, the circumference of my border expands endlessly, and the limits of my individuality become vague. And in this condition, writing emerged as a consequence of my observations. In this repetition, anxiety and loneliness and ennui became the metaphysics of my poetry. I pretended to be writing about a homeless person, but I was, in fact, writing about myself. I pretended to be writing about Mozart, but I was, in fact, writing about myself. I pretend to be writing about a dog wandering the city streets, but I was, in fact, writing about myself. I pretended to be writing about myself, but I was writing about another me, all the way down there at the bottom—I was writing about the bottom itself. My writing self is already a written life. This is how I am reconstructing it.

If we call this work poetry, then poetry will get mad. If we call this prose, prose will get mad. Poetry rises higher than this, and prose reaches and spreads to lower places. This is minus-poetry, minus-prose. I wondered if I should call this not-poetry-not-prose, or better yet *shisanmun*, poetry-prose, because I felt I was insulting both poetry and prose if I called my work either of those things. I thought, maybe I should call them recited prose, or mumbled poetry. I have always thought that there are things only poetry can express, and things only prose can express. However, this time I wanted to invent a genre that hangs between those two genres. These words were written by someone who gets more anxious the more they observe themselves. These words are the words of a person who is the personification of ennui and loneliness. These words are the words of the one who called such a person "I." These words don't have genres; instead, they are written in longing for the country of poetry that exists far away in the unknown, in the constellation furthest from Aerok, the mere thought of which causes vertigo. There are pieces in this collection that are like poems, and there are pieces that are like prose poems, and there are pieces that feel like vignettes. I held onto the tension between Kim Su-young, who said that he wrote poetry like he was writing a novel, and Baudelaire, who said that he wrote poetry even when he was writing prose. I resolved not to fall into the ecstasy of holiness, the self-abuse of pity, and that deception called morality.

MARCH 2016
Kim Hyesoon

ARTIST'S AFTERWORD

Often, when drawings are presented next to words, they are thought of as representations or interpretations of the words. Often, they are treated as mere illustrations inspired by the words. However, these drawings here are not artistic representations of the words. I want to reveal that these drawings existed before the words. I selected from many of my existing drawings and placed a few of them next to the words. I thought it would be nice if there was a 'chemistry' between the two.

I drew as if writing a daily diary. When I sought sleep after finishing my day, a certain 'transformation' time came upon me, as if hypnagogic imagery was projected between sleep and reality. As midnight neared, a 'time' called my day, experienced with gestures, sensations, and language, visited me, clothed in materiality, manifesting as a shape. I quickly sketched out this form, one of the transformations of time. I might even call these sketches records of sensations' content that surprised me throughout my day. As my diary entries piled up, I sensed with my 'diary-like shapes' what Paul Crutzen called the fourth Holocene, the Anthropocene, in which humanity's rapid expansion is radically changing life itself at an incredible speed. My shapes seemed like aliens formed between the visible and the invisible world. I gave names to these shapes and came to think that I was going through an age called Leeficene.

MARCH 2016
Fi Jae Lee